Teacher Guide

VOCABULARY

word meaning, pronunciation, prefixes, suffixes, synonyms, antonyms, and fun!

in Action

LOYOLA PRESS.

Chicago

LOYOLA PRESS.

3441 N. Ashland Avenue
Chicago, Illinois 60657
(800) 621-1008
www.loyolapress.com

Cover & Interior Art: Anni Betts
Cover Design: Judine O'Shea
Interior Design: Kathy Greenholdt and Joan Bledig

Copyright © 2010 Loyola Press

Manufactured in the United States of America.

ISBN-10: 0-8294-2779-1
ISBN-13: 978-0-8294-2779-0

12 13 14 15 16 17 Hess 10 9 8 6 7 5 4 3

VISIT
www.vocabularyinaction.com
ACCESS CODE: **VTB-8994**

Contents

Pronunciation Key

This key shows the meanings of the abbreviations and symbols used throughout the book.

Some English words have more than one possible pronunciation. This book gives only one pronunciation per word, except when different pronunciations indicate different parts of speech. For example, when the word *relay* is used as a noun, it is pronounced rē´ lā; as a verb, the word is pronounced rə lā´.

Parts of Speech

adj.	adjective	*int.*	interjection	*prep.*	preposition
adv.	adverb	*n.*	noun	*part.*	participle
				v.	verb

Vowels

ā	tape	ə	about, circus	ôr	torn
a	map	ī	kite	oi	noise
âr	stare	i	win	ou	foul
ä	car, father	ō	toe	o͞o	soon
ē	meet	o	mop	o͝o	book
e	kept	ô	law	u	tug

Consonants

ch	check	ŋ	rang	y	yellow
g	girl	th	thimble	zh	treasure
j	jam	th̶	that	sh	shelf

Stress

The accent mark follows the syllable receiving the major stress, such as in the word *plaster* (plas´ tər).

Introduction

Vocabulary in Action is the premier vocabulary development program that increases students' literacy skills and improves test scores.

Researchers and educators agree that vocabulary development is essential in learning how to communicate effectively through listening, speaking, reading, and writing. The National Reading Panel (2000) has identified vocabulary as one of the five areas that increase students' reading ability. After the third grade, reading difficulties are often attributed to a vocabulary deficit—an inability to understand word meaning.

Vocabulary in Action offers the following elements to help students develop this critical literacy skill:

- Flexible leveling and student placement for individualized instruction

- Words that were researched and selected specifically for frequency, occurrence, and relevance to assessment and everyday life

- Intentional, direct instruction focused on words and their meanings, usage, and relationships to other words

- Repeated word appearance in a variety of contexts for extensive exposure and practice with literal and figurative meanings

- Application of new vocabulary skills through practice exercises, assessments, and standardized test preparation opportunities

Program Overview

Each Student Book includes

- **Program Pretest** to identify level of understanding

- **Research-based Word Lists** selected for frequency, occurrence, and relevance to assessment

- **One Hundred or More Related Words** including synonyms and antonyms

- **Word Pronunciations, Meanings, and Identifications of Parts of Speech**

- **At Least a Dozen Activities per Chapter**, including activities for words in context, word meaning, word usage, related words, and word building

- **Challenge Words and Activities**

- **Fun with Words** activities for additional practice

- **Test-Taking Tips** section covering test-taking skills, testing formats, and study of testing vocabulary including classic roots, prefixes, and suffixes

- **Special Features** for etymology, mnemonic devices, historical facts, word trivia, and word origin

- **Notable Quotes** that show words in context

- **Chapter Review Assessments** for multiple chapters

- **Program Posttest** to determine overall growth

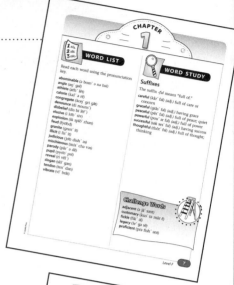

Total Vocabulary Word Count by Level

LEVEL	WORDS TO KNOW	ADDITIONAL WORDS
D	150	over 100
E	225	over 150
F, G, H	375	over 200

Each Teacher Guide includes

- **Annotated Guide** similar to the student book for easy correction

- **Additional Games and Activities** for a variety of groupings, learning styles, multiple intelligences, and levels of proficiency in English

- **Suggestions for Guided and Independent Practice**

- **Academic Language Practice** with games and activities, including work with classic roots

- **Icons** for easy identification

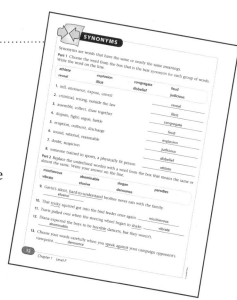

The *Vocabulary in Action* Web site includes

- Assessments

- Pretests and Reviews

- Word Lists and Definitions

- Vocabulary Games

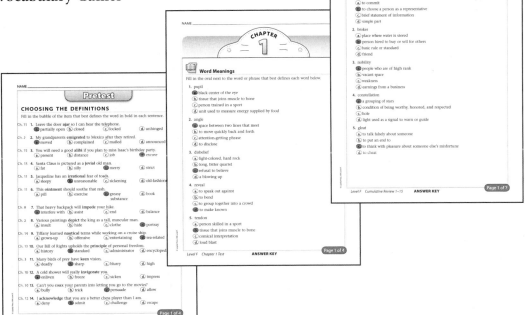

www.vocabularyinaction.com

How to Implement This Program

With *Vocabulary in Action*, it is easy to differentiate instruction to meet the needs of all students.

Student Placement

Use the following chart to help determine the book most appropriate for each individual student. Differences in level include word difficulty, sentence complexity, and ideas presented in context. In addition to the chart, consider a student's achievement level on any pretest that you give. Adjust books based on a student's achievement on a pretest and other vocabulary assignments, his or her ability to retain new information, and the student's overall work ethic and interest level.

Placement Levels

Typical Grade-Level Assignments		Accelerated Grade-Level Assignments	
LEVEL	**GRADE**	**LEVEL**	**GRADE**
D	4	D	3
E	5	E	4
F	6	F	5
G	7	G	6
H	8	H	7

To Begin

At the beginning of the year, choose a book for each student based on the above criteria. Have each student take the program pretest in his or her book. Avoid timing the test. Give students enough time to complete the test thoughtfully and with confidence. After grading the test and noting student achievement levels, make book adjustments if necessary.

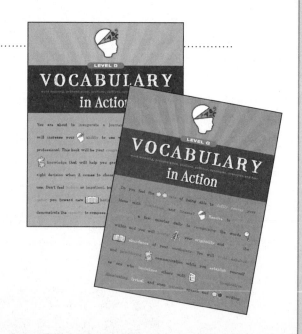

Work Through the Chapters

Follow these steps to implement each chapter.

1. **Chapter opener:** Have students work with partners, in small groups, or with you to read aloud each word in the **Word List.** Check pronunciation and discuss the definition of each word, having students find the words in a dictionary if you have time. Have students review the **Word Study** section. Introduce the **Challenge Words** in the same way as the Word List. Then have students remove the page and complete the back side.

2. **Chapter pages:** Based on students' confidence and ability, assign students to complete chapter activities independently, with you, with peers, or as homework. Students should complete activities for Words in Context, Word Meanings, Use Your Vocabulary, Word Learning, Synonyms, Antonyms, Word Study, Challenge Words, and Fun with Words. Provide support through modeling and discussion. Here are some approaches:

   - Teacher presents and completes a page with students during the first 10 or 15 minutes of each reading or language arts session. Pages are reviewed simultaneously as guided practice.

   - Students complete chapter pages in class after other reading or language arts assignments are complete. Pages are collected and reviewed after class.

   - Students complete chapter pages as homework assignments, one page per night. Pages are collected and reviewed after completion.

3. **Reteaching/additional practice:** Monitor student progress on a regular basis. If students need additional practice, use the **Games & Activities** on pages 189–194 of this guide or the **Teacher Activities** on pages 195–196.

4. **Standardized test preparation:** At least one month prior to standardized testing, work with students to complete pages 183–184.

5. **Chapter reviews:** After completing every three chapters, administer the Chapter Review to note students' progress and to identify difficult words.

6. **Assessment:** Have students complete a formal assessment after each chapter. Visit **www.vocabularyinaction.com** and access the assessment with this code: **VTB-8994.** You can also access a **Pretest** and **Review.**

Sample Yearly Plan for Level F

Following is one way to implement *Vocabulary in Action* for Level F.

WEEK	STUDENT BOOK	RELATED ACTIVITIES	
1	Pretest		
2–3	Chapter 1	Games & Activities (pp. 189–194) Teacher Activities (pp. 195–196)	Chapter 1 Assessment
4–5	Chapter 2	Games & Activities (pp. 189–194) Teacher Activities (pp. 195–196)	Chapter 2 Assessment
6–7	Chapter 3	Games & Activities (pp. 189–194) Teacher Activities (pp. 195–196)	Chapter 3 Assessment
8	Review Chapters 1–3	Online Games (www.vocabularyinaction.com) Cumulative Review	
9–10	Chapter 4	Games & Activities (pp. 189–194) Teacher Activities (pp. 195–196)	Chapter 4 Assessment
11–12	Chapter 5	Games & Activities (pp. 189–194) Teacher Activities (pp. 195–196)	Chapter 5 Assessment
13–14	Chapter 6	Games & Activities (pp. 189–194) Teacher Activities (pp. 195–196)	Chapter 6 Assessment
15	Review Chapters 4–6	Online Games (www.vocabularyinaction.com) Cumulative Review	
16–17	Chapter 7	Games & Activities (pp. 189–194) Teacher Activities (pp. 195–196)	Chapter 7 Assessment
18–19	Chapter 8	Games & Activities (pp. 189–194) Teacher Activities (pp. 195–196)	Chapter 8 Assessment
20–21	Chapter 9	Games & Activities (pp. 189–194) Teacher Activities (pp. 195–196)	Chapter 9 Assessment
22	Review Chapters 7–9	Online Games (www.vocabularyinaction.com) Cumulative Review	
23	Chapter 10	Games & Activities (pp. 189–194) Teacher Activities (pp. 195–196)	Chapter 10 Assessment
24–25	Chapter 11	Games & Activities (pp. 189–194) Teacher Activities (pp. 195–196)	Chapter 11 Assessment
26–27	Chapter 12	Games & Activities (pp. 189–194) Teacher Activities (pp. 195–196)	Chapter 12 Assessment
28	Review Chapters 10–12	Online Games (www.vocabularyinaction.com) Cumulative Review	
29	Chapter 13	Games & Activities (pp. 189–194) Teacher Activities (pp. 195–196)	Chapter 13 Assessment
30–31	Chapter 14	Games & Activities (pp. 189–194) Teacher Activities (pp. 195–196)	Chapter 14 Assessment
32–33	Chapter 15	Games & Activities (pp. 189–194) Teacher Activities (pp. 195–196)	Chapter 15 Assessment
34	Review Chapters 13–15	Online Games (www.vocabularyinaction.com) Cumulative Review	
35	Posttest		

Pretest

This test contains some of the words you will find in this book. It will give you an idea of the kinds of words you will study. When you have completed all the units, the posttest will measure what you have learned.

CHOOSING THE DEFINITIONS

Fill in the bubble of the item that best defines the word in bold in each sentence.

Ch. 1 1. On cool evenings, the campers **congregate** around the campfire.
a. dance **b.** gather **c.** cook **d.** sing

Ch. 1 2. Samuel thought a Saturday job would be a **judicious** use of his time.
a. wise **b.** wasteful **c.** silly **d.** dangerous

Ch. 14 3. Jennifer stopped the car so everyone could admire the **scenic** view.
a. colorful **b.** ugly **c.** desert **d.** attractive

Ch. 2 4. Washing dishes is a **tedious** chore.
a. exciting **b.** old **c.** boring **d.** brilliant

Ch. 3 5. Taking shorter showers **conserves** water.
a. drinks **b.** uses **c.** saves **d.** heats

Ch. 2 6. The class president will **abstain** from voting if her sister runs for office.
a. avoid **b.** lead **c.** encourage **d.** count

Ch.3 7. The flu makes you feel awful, but it is not a **terminal** illness.
a. short **b.** mild **c.** horrible **d.** deadly

Ch. 5 8. Lying by the warm fire, Robert gave a sigh of **contentment**.
a. sadness **b.** happiness **c.** disgust **d.** exhaustion

Ch. 8 9. Swimming across the lake takes a great deal of **stamina**.
a. lessons **b.** speed **c.** endurance **d.** nourishment

Ch. 5 10. During the earthquake, the statue slid off its **pedestal** and broke.
a. hill **b.** museum **c.** base **d.** frame

Ch. 5 11. Amanda felt a sense of **triumph** after she scored the final goal.
a. victory **b.** defeat **c.** happiness **d.** anger

Ch. 15 12. The police assured the witness that her name would be kept **confidential**.
a. public **b.** secret **c.** rewarded **d.** misspelled

Ch. 6 13. Even though it was late, Sydney felt an **obligation** to attend the meeting.
a. desire **b.** promise **c.** duty **d.** invitation

Ch. 7 **14.** Our canoe ride through the river's rapids was **adventurous**.
    (a.) dull   **(b.)** tiring   **(c.)** lengthy   **(d.)** risky

Ch. 4 **15.** I **despise** spinach, but I eat it because it's so good for me.
    (a.) grow   **(b.)** hate   **(c.)** crave   **(d.)** digest

Ch. 7 **16.** Bad-smelling **gaseous** clouds poured out of the factory's smokestack.
    (a.) solid   **(b.)** formless   **(c.)** heavy   **(d.)** dangerous

Ch. 7 **17.** Vines had grown up to **obscure** the entrance to the abandoned farmhouse.
    (a.) hide   **(b.)** light   **(c.)** destroy   **(d.)** decorate

Ch. 1 **18.** The **feud** between the two families continued for years.
    (a.) fence   **(b.)** friendship   **(c.)** relationship   **(d.)** dispute

Ch. 7 **19.** The new police cadets pledged to **uphold** the law.
    (a.) break   **(b.)** write   **(c.)** follow   **(d.)** learn

Ch. 8 **20.** The room was at the end of a long, dark **corridor**.
    (a.) road   **(b.)** sidewalk   **(c.)** tunnel   **(d.)** hallway

Ch. 3 **21.** My clever **disguise** even fooled my mom.
    (a.) answer   **(b.)** mask   **(c.)** lie   **(d.)** outfit

Ch. 8 **22.** Kyle thought the prank was harmless, but it **enraged** his best friend.
    (a.) angered   **(b.)** thrilled   **(c.)** scared   **(d.)** amused

Ch. 9 **23.** At the grand opening, a **horde** of customers waited outside the mall doors.
    (a.) crowd   **(b.)** couple   **(c.)** family   **(d.)** small group

Ch. 6 **24.** Morgan is a star basketball player but an **inept** baseball player.
    (a.) capable   **(b.)** better   **(c.)** clumsy   **(d.)** average

Ch. 9 **25.** Nicole went to the manager's office to **inquire** about the summer job.
    (a.) complain   **(b.)** ask   **(c.)** study   **(d.)** think

Ch. 9 **26.** The toddler didn't **shed** a tear when he fell off his tricycle.
    (a.) cause   **(b.)** wipe off   **(c.)** pour out   **(d.)** hold back

Ch. 4 **27.** Steven was **appreciative** of his big brother's help.
    (a.) thankful   **(b.)** critical   **(c.)** ungrateful   **(d.)** bothered

Ch. 10 **28.** We can accomplish the difficult task with hard work and **determination**.
    (a.) humor   **(b.)** speed   **(c.)** purpose   **(d.)** fear

Ch. 10 **29.** Jasmine was **distraught** until her lost MP3 player was returned.
    (a.) satisfied   **(b.)** upset   **(c.)** encouraged   **(d.)** pleased

Ch. 2 **30.** The events that followed were the **consequence** of Connor's angry words.
- **a.** argument
- **b.** beginning
- **c.** work
- **d.** result

Ch. 10 **31.** After making an error in the big game, Grace felt **humiliation** for days.
- **a.** shame
- **b.** joy
- **c.** anger
- **d.** pride

Ch. 10 **32.** The scientist planned to research **marine** life.
- **a.** space
- **b.** desert
- **c.** underground
- **d.** sea

Ch. 6 **33.** Before she could try the recipe, the chef had to **convert** the metric measurements.
- **a.** read
- **b.** change
- **c.** gather
- **d.** test

Ch. 10 **34.** When Tim's cat began behaving **oddly**, he made an appointment with the vet.
- **a.** nicely
- **b.** strangely
- **c.** angrily
- **d.** safely

Ch. 10 **35.** The **shrill** sound of the siren hurt everyone's ears.
- **a.** drawn-out
- **b.** loud
- **c.** high-pitched
- **d.** low

Ch. 5 **36.** Sierra felt it was her **destiny** to become a doctor.
- **a.** future
- **b.** bad luck
- **c.** career
- **d.** ambition

Ch. 10 **37.** The sailors went out in spite of the forecast of **variable** winds.
- **a.** north
- **b.** strong
- **c.** light
- **d.** changeable

Ch. 11 **38.** Sara's feelings were hurt by her parents' **criticism**.
- **a.** description
- **b.** disapproval
- **c.** summary
- **d.** contents

Ch. 9 **39.** When the students worked together, they were able to **generate** more ideas.
- **a.** talk
- **b.** criticize
- **c.** produce
- **d.** destroy

Ch. 11 **40.** In math class, we learned how to measure the **diameter** of a circle.
- **a.** distance around
- **b.** weight
- **c.** distance across
- **d.** density

Ch. 11 **41.** School was closed for a week because of an **epidemic** of measles.
- **a.** outbreak
- **b.** symptoms
- **c.** vaccine
- **d.** end

Ch. 2 **42.** The sleeping lion looks peaceful, but it can be a **fierce** enemy.
- **a.** tame
- **b.** huge
- **c.** proud
- **d.** furious

Ch. 11 **43.** Charles thought he would **prevail** over his opponent in the karate match.
- **a.** win
- **b.** throw
- **c.** stand
- **d.** lose

Ch. 11 **44.** I thought I spotted a flaw in the cloth, but it was just a **variation** in its texture.
- **a.** similarity
- **b.** lump
- **c.** difference
- **d.** smoothness

Ch. 1 **45.** At first, we thought Olivia's **mischievous** behavior was cute.
- **a.** pleasant
- **b.** naughty
- **c.** affectionate
- **d.** foolish

Ch. 11 46. In its early years, people thought the telephone was a **wondrous** invention.
(a.) shocking　　(b.) frightening　　(c.) useful　　(d.) amazing

Ch. 12 47. We planned a celebration to **commemorate** Mrs. Jarzab's teaching career.
(a.) honor　　(b.) discredit　　(c.) ignore　　(d.) write down

Ch. 6 48. The novel's main character turned out to be a real **scoundrel**.
(a.) hero　　(b.) villain　　(c.) star　　(d.) pilot

Ch. 12 49. We finally had to tell Isaiah that his tasteless jokes made him a **bore**.
(a.) woodpecker　　(b.) wild pig　　(c.) dull person　　(d.) comedian

Ch. 12 50. Last summer's **drought** ruined the farmers' crops.
(a.) storm　　(b.) dry spell　　(c.) fire　　(d.) dirt road

Ch. 4 51. Once in a while it's good to take a **solitary** walk to think things over.
(a.) brisk　　(b.) long　　(c.) friendly　　(d.) alone

Ch. 12 52. I wish my sister would not **gloat** about her grades all the time.
(a.) boast　　(b.) talk　　(c.) whine　　(d.) worry

Ch. 12 53. After Kimberly's description, I had a good **mental** picture of her hometown.
(a.) physical　　(b.) of the mouth　　(c.) masculine　　(d.) of the mind

Ch. 3 54. The driving instructor told us not to **accelerate** too quickly.
(a.) stop　　(b.) slow down　　(c.) speed up　　(d.) drive

Ch. 12 55. The sprinkling ban was in effect because of the low level of the **reservoir**.
(a.) savings account　(b.) grass　　(c.) water supply　　(d.) valley

Ch. 12 56. We let the gravy **simmer** while we prepared the salad.
(a.) thicken　　(b.) heat　　(c.) stir　　(d.) season

Ch. 2 57. Before I went onstage, I had a few **qualms** about singing for an audience.
(a.) dreams　　(b.) songs　　(c.) surprises　　(d.) worries

Ch. 12 58. Our **sturdy** canvas tents kept us dry during the thunderstorm.
(a.) strong　　(b.) scratchy　　(c.) thin　　(d.) ugly

Ch. 13 59. My mother has a successful career as a jewelry **broker**.
(a.) manufacturer　(b.) designer　　(c.) model　　(d.) salesperson

Ch. 5 60. Jack likes to spend his **leisure** time building models.
(a.) class　　(b.) free　　(c.) work　　(d.) evening

Ch. 13 61. It was time for the ceremony to **commence**, but the speaker was late.
(a.) end　　(b.) continue　　(c.) begin　　(d.) perform

Ch. 13 **62.** The author **dedicated** the book to all the students at King School.
    (a.) wrote   (b.) devoted   (c.) read aloud   (d.) mailed

Ch. 7 **63.** Mackenzie enjoys using the computer to **correspond** with her friends.
    (a.) spy   (b.) work   (c.) play   (d.) communicate

Ch. 13 **64.** The club's fundraising plan **evolved** from one member's casual comment.
    (a.) turned   (b.) discouraged   (c.) developed   (d.) ended

Ch. 13 **65.** The president received an **ovation** when he stepped up to the microphone.
    (a.) army   (b.) applause   (c.) invitation   (d.) shock

Ch. 1 **66.** A skunk protects itself with its **abominable** odor.
    (a.) offensive   (b.) fragrant   (c.) delightful   (d.) strong

Ch. 13 **67.** A **submissive** dog is easily trained.
    (a.) mean   (b.) friendly   (c.) large   (d.) obedient

Ch. 14 **68.** When his friends knocked, Gabriel hurried to **conceal** the dirty dishes.
    (a.) scrub   (b.) hide   (c.) throw away   (d.) show off

Ch. 6 **69.** Waves caused by a hurricane can be even more **destructive** than the wind.
    (a.) beautiful   (b.) powerful   (c.) creative   (d.) damaging

Ch. 14 **70.** Beavers **gnaw** on trees until they fall.
    (a.) scrape   (b.) kick   (c.) chew   (d.) break

Ch. 14 **71.** The accident was caused by a **negligent** worker.
    (a.) well-trained   (b.) tired   (c.) careless   (d.) serious

Ch. 4 **72.** The principal promised to **consider** the new rule.
    (a.) think about   (b.) carry out   (c.) enforce   (d.) overturn

Ch. 14 **73.** The accountant was able to **swindle** her trusting business partners.
    (a.) praise   (b.) leave   (c.) work for   (d.) cheat

Ch. 15 **74.** Each class sent a **delegate** to the school meeting.
    (a.) gathering   (b.) representative   (c.) vote   (d.) speaker

Ch. 14 **75.** Jared made a **gruesome** mask to wear in the play.
    (a.) gorgeous   (b.) frightening   (c.) new   (d.) artistic

Ch. 15 **76.** The graph showed a **gradual** increase in grocery prices.
    (a.) large   (b.) expected   (c.) slow   (d.) sudden

Ch. 15 **77.** During World War II, some countries remained **neutral**.
    (a.) uninvolved   (b.) wealthy   (c.) angry   (d.) unfair

Ch. 8 78. The new student seemed **timid** until we got to know her.
    a. nasty   **b.** shy   **c.** unhappy   **d.** intelligent

Ch. 15 79. **Technical** books about computers are often difficult to understand.
    a. simple   **b.** long   **c.** scientific   **d.** expensive

Ch. 4 80. His father warned Sean not to **trifle** with his little brother's feelings.
    a. wrestle   **b.** treat carelessly   **c.** discuss   **d.** argue with

Ch. 9 81. Sophia needs time to **recuperate** from the accident, but she will be fine.
    a. get sick   **b.** sleep   **c.** get well   **d.** run

Ch. 8 82. The colonists decided it was time to **rebel** against the unfair government.
    a. reject authority   **b.** obey authority   **c.** celebrate   **d.** pay taxes

Ch.8 83. In solving the conflict, Hailey displayed a real talent for **persuasion**.
    a. giving speeches   **b.** writing essays   **c.** convincing   **d.** fighting

Ch. 15 84. Our new neighbor's **jovial** smile gave us a clue to his personality.
    a. sinister   **b.** nervous   **c.** shy   **d.** merry

Ch. 9 85. Our class wrote a letter about the problem to the town **council**.
    a. mayor   **b.** city hall   **c.** treasurer   **d.** board of
                                                                    advisors

Ch. 11 86. We didn't realize that the window was **ajar** until we felt a cold draft.
    a. broken   **b.** dirty   **c.** open   **d.** locked

Ch. 5 87. No matter what we did, we could not make the poster **adhere** to the wall.
    a. cling   **b.** fall off   **c.** look good   **d.** draw

Ch. 10 88. When the electricity shut down, the emergency **generator** saved the day.
    a. employee   **b.** director   **c.** power supply   **d.** rescue team

Ch. 11 89. The **geologist** who explored the sea valley brought up some rare specimens.
    a. submarine   **b.** animal scientist   **c.** rock scientist   **d.** mapmaker

Ch. 5 90. Luis was voted the best **scholar** in the class.
    a. artist   **b.** athlete   **c.** teacher   **d.** student

CHAPTER 1

WORD LIST

Read each word using the pronunciation key.

abominable (ə bom´ ə nə bəl)
angle (aŋ´ gəl)
athlete (ath´ lēt)
calorie (kal´ ə rē)
congregate (koŋ´ gri gāt)
denounce (di nouns´)
disbelief (dis bi lēf´)
elusive (i lōō´ siv)
explosion (ik splō´ zhən)
feud (fyōōd)
granite (gran´ it)
illicit (i lis´ it)
judicious (jōō dish´ əs)
mischievous (mis´ chə vəs)
parody (pâr´ ə dē)
pupil (pyōō´ pəl)
reveal (ri vēl´)
slogan (slō´ gən)
tendon (ten´ dən)
vibrate (vī´ brāt)

WORD STUDY

Suffixes

The suffix *-ful* means "full of."

careful (kâr´ fəl) *(adj.)* full of care or concern
graceful (grās´ fəl) *(adj.)* having grace
peaceful (pēs´ fəl) *(adj.)* full of peace; quiet
powerful (pou´ ər fəl) *(adj.)* full of power
successful (sək ses´ fəl) *(adj.)* having success
thoughtful (thôt´ fəl) *(adj.)* full of thought; thinking

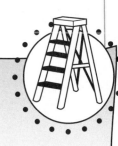

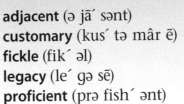

Challenge Words

adjacent (ə jā´ sənt)
customary (kus´ tə mâr ē)
fickle (fik´ əl)
legacy (le´ gə sē)
proficient (prə fish´ ənt)

■ **TEACHER TIP:** See page ix for suggestions on how to use this page.

Read each sentence below to figure out the meaning of the word in **bold**. Use reasoning skills and the remainder of the sentence to help you. Write the meaning of the word on the line.

1. Emily, a natural **athlete**, ran every day to prepare for the marathon.

   a person trained or skilled in a sport

2. The detective uncovered the criminal's **illicit** activities and arrested him.

   unauthorized; unlawful; illegal

3. The sudden **explosion** at the factory blew out the windows and doors.

   a loud blast; a blowing up

4. Where will we **congregate** before the concert so we can go in together?

   to group together

5. Did Jacob **reveal** his identity before the masquerade party?

   to make known; to disclose

6. The courthouse steps are made of **granite** taken from an Alabama rock quarry.

   a hard rock, usually pink or gray, used for building

7. When hiking in the desert, a careful and **judicious** use of water is necessary.

   sensible; wise

8. Can we settle our disagreement now instead of turning it into a long family **feud**?

   an extended and bitter quarrel

9. My **mischievous** sister played a practical joke on Anna.

   causing mischief, naughty

10. I need a good, catchy **slogan** to write on my campaign posters.

   an attention-getting word or phrase

WORD MEANINGS

Word Learning

Within each group, study the spelling, part(s) of speech, and meaning(s) of each word. Complete each sentence by writing the word on the line. Then read the sentence.

1. **abominable** *(adj.)* 1. offensive; 2. unpleasant

   Can someone stop that screaming child's _____abominable_____ behavior?

2. **angle** *(n.)* the space between two surfaces or lines that meet; *(v.)* to bend at an angle

   Each corner of a square is a right _____angle_____.

   If you _____angle_____ the ladder more toward the house, it will reach the roof.

3. **athlete** *(n.)* a person trained or skilled in a sport

   Who do you think is baseball's best _____athlete_____?

4. **calorie** *(n.)* a unit used to measure the energy supplied by food

   That diet drink claims to have only one _____calorie_____.

5. **congregate** *(v.)* to group together into a crowd

   The early students always _____congregate_____ at the school's entrance.

6. **denounce** *(v.)* to strongly speak out against someone or something

   Our committee will appear before Congress to _____denounce_____ violence on TV.

7. **disbelief** *(n.)* reluctance or refusal to believe

   "Are you telling me you saw a flying saucer?" Julia said in _____disbelief_____.

8. **elusive** *(adj.)* difficult to describe or understand

   Some say there's an _____elusive_____ fragrance around the old, abandoned factory.

9. **explosion** *(n.)* 1. a loud blast; 2. a blowing up

   Smoking rubble was all that remained after the _____explosion_____.

10. **feud** *(n.)* 1. an extended and bitter quarrel between families; 2. an extreme hatred between people or groups; *(v.)* to carry on a violent quarrel over an extended period of time

    The _____feud_____ over land continued for generations.

    Do you think the sisters will _____feud_____ over possession of the computer?

11. **granite** *(n.)* a hard rock, usually pink or gray, used for building

    The new park statue is made of _____granite_____ taken from these hills.

12. **illicit** *(adj.)* 1. unauthorized; 2. unlawful; 3. illegal

    Security cameras recorded the _____illicit_____ activity of the managers.

13. **judicious** *(adj.)* 1. sensible; 2. wise; 3. having or using good judgment

    The mayor's _____judicious_____ actions avoided an embarrassing mistake.

14. **mischievous** *(adj.)* 1. causing mischief; naughty; 2. harmful; 3. prankish

    The court jester's _____mischievous_____ deeds did not please the king.

15. **parody** *(n.)* a comical interpretation of a musical or literary work

    Benjamin's _____parody_____ of that song got us all laughing.

16. **pupil** *(n.)* the area that is black in the center of the eye

    Those eyedrops caused Seth's _____pupil_____ to enlarge.

17. **reveal** *(v.)* 1. to make known; 2. to disclose; 3. to publicize or broadcast

    Bailey will _____reveal_____ the $10,000 winner during the football game.

18. **slogan** *(n.)* an attention-getting word or phrase used by a business, political party, or group

    Help me come up with a catchy _____slogan_____ for our charity.

19. **tendon** *(n.)* a strong band of tissue in the body that joins muscle to bone

    The pitcher pulled a leg _____tendon_____ and won't be playing today.

20. **vibrate** *(v.)* to move quickly back and forth

    We could feel the roller coaster shake and _____vibrate_____ as we rounded the curve.

Use Your Vocabulary

Choose the word from the Word List that best completes each sentence. Write the word on the line. You may use the plural form of nouns and the past tense of verbs if necessary.

This morning, as I was eating a low-fat breakfast of 70 __1__ , my father __2__ his special, secret plan. At first he gave only __3__ hints that we didn't understand. "I have made a wise, __4__ decision that I think you will like," Dad claimed. "To avoid the yearly __5__ over our vacation plans, I have already made the arrangements."

My sister and I looked at each other in __6__ . Usually, we discussed plans as a family. "Before you __7__ the plans, listen first and see if you can guess our plan," Dad said. "I have not used our vacation money in any wrongful or __8__ way," he said. "To begin, we will all __9__ at a large building made of gray __10__ just outside our city. We will walk long distances in this building, so we'll need to stretch our leg __11__ like a(n) __12__ to get into good, physical shape.

"Outside the building are straight roadways that form __13__ . The vehicles on these roadways usually __14__ and shake as they take off, but our takeoff will be gentle and nearly silent. We'll be in our own Friendly Skies, to quote a well-known __15__ ." He sang a quick, funny __16__ of the song "Up, up and away in my beautiful balloon."

"It sounds like a(n) __17__ beginning to our vacation," my sister groaned.

"Dad, stop your __18__ teasing!" I said. "You're talking about the airport."

The __19__ of my sister's eyes grew larger as she realized that there might be more to this vacation than she thought. "Yes," said Dad. "We're going to the airport for a journey in a hot air balloon." The silence in the room was like the silence that follows a loud __20__ . Then we cheered.

1. _____ calories
2. _____ revealed
3. _____ elusive
4. _____ judicious
5. _____ feud
6. _____ disbelief
7. _____ denounce
8. _____ illicit
9. _____ congregate
10. _____ granite
11. _____ tendons
12. _____ athlete
13. _____ angles
14. _____ vibrate
15. _____ slogan
16. _____ parody
17. _____ abominable
18. _____ mischievous
19. _____ pupils
20. _____ explosion

SYNONYMS

Synonyms are words that have the same or nearly the same meanings.

Part 1 Choose the word from the box that is the best synonym for each group of words. Write the word on the line.

athlete	explosion	congregate	feud
reveal	illicit	disbelief	judicious

1. tell, announce, expose, unveil   _____reveal_____

2. criminal, wrong, outside the law   _____illicit_____

3. assemble, collect, draw together   _____congregate_____

4. dispute, fight; argue, battle   _____feud_____

5. eruption, outburst, discharge   _____explosion_____

6. sound, rational, reasonable   _____judicious_____

7. doubt, suspicion   _____disbelief_____

8. someone trained in sports, a physically fit person   _____athlete_____

Part 2 Replace the underlined word(s) with a word from the box that means the same or almost the same. Write your answer on the line.

mischievous	abominable	slogan	parodies
vibrate	elusive	denounce	

9. Gavin's silent, <u>hard-to-understand</u> brother never eats with the family.
_____elusive_____

10. That <u>tricky</u> squirrel got into the bird feeder once again. _____mischievous_____

11. Travis pulled over when the steering wheel began to <u>shake</u>. _____vibrate_____

12. Diana expected the boys to be <u>horrible</u> dancers, but they weren't.
_____abominable_____

13. Choose your words carefully when you <u>speak against</u> your campaign opponent's viewpoint. _____denounce_____

14. The comedy was a <u>funny version</u> of several different summer movies.

_____parody_____

15. Brett can't get that car dealer's <u>saying</u> out of his head. _____slogan_____

 **ANTONYMS**

Antonyms are words that have opposite or nearly opposite meanings.

Part 1 Choose the word from the box that is the antonym for each group of words. Write the word on the line.

| judicious | vibrate | elusive | denounce | congregate |

1. disperse, leave, scatter   _____congregate_____

2. clear, well known, easy to define   _____elusive_____

3. praise, support, approve   _____denounce_____

4. silly, foolish, senseless   _____judicious_____

5. still, motionless, at rest   _____vibrate_____

Vocabulary in Action

Jack Roosevelt "Jackie" Robinson was a husband, soldier, and civil rights activist. He was also an excellent **athlete** who ran track and played baseball, basketball, and football in college. On April 15, 1947, he became more than a great athlete. That day, Jackie Robinson became the first African American to play for a Major League Baseball team. When Robinson put on his #42 Brooklyn Dodgers uniform and stepped onto the field, he ended 80 years of baseball segregation. Today, Americans celebrate April 15 as Jackie Robinson Day to honor the athlete whose courage and tenacity helped end the shameful practice of segregation in baseball.

Part 2 Replace the underlined word(s) with a word from the box that means the opposite or almost the opposite. Write your answer on the line.

disbelief	abominable	illicit	reveal	feud

6. "Look! I got an A on my reading test," Erika said with <u>confidence</u>.

      disbelief
     _____

7. The twins <u>get along well</u> all the time, and this astonishes their parents.

      feud
     _____

8. Edgar sent me the most <u>attractive</u> orange skirt I have ever seen.

      abominable
     _____

9. In some states, burning autumn leaves is <u>legal</u>. _____illicit_____

10. The news reporter plans to <u>conceal</u> harmful information. _____reveal_____

WORD STUDY

Suffixes Write the word from the box that has the same meaning as the first word(s) and the suffix *-ful*.

powerful	graceful	peaceful
successful	careful	thoughtful

1. concern + ful   _____careful_____

2. quiet + ful   _____peaceful_____

3. idea + ful   _____thoughtful_____

4. beauty of movement + ful   _____graceful_____

5. strength + ful   _____powerful_____

6. fortune + ful   _____successful_____

CHALLENGE WORDS

Word Learning—Challenge!

Study the spelling, part of speech, and meaning(s) of each word. Complete each sentence by writing the word on the line. Then read the sentence.

1. **adjacent** *(adj.)* 1. having a common border; 2. directly preceding or following

   Room 201 and Room 202 are _____adjacent_____ rooms.

2. **customary** *(adj.)* commonly practiced or used

   Every morning I eat my _____customary_____ bowl of cereal and fruit.

3. **fickle** *(adj.)* 1. easily gives in to change; 2. lacks consistency

   I seem to have _____fickle_____ friends who change their minds all the time.

4. **legacy** *(n.)* something received from an ancestor

   My love for African history is part of the _____legacy_____ of my Great-Uncle Martin.

5. **proficient** *(adj.)* having competence and skill in a specific area

   Desiree is a _____proficient_____ basketball player.

Use Your Vocabulary—Challenge!

The Search An ancestor of yours has left a large trunk buried somewhere. You find a map, follow it, and uncover the trunk. On a separate sheet of paper, write for a magazine an account of your search. Use the Challenge Words above. Be sure to tell where you went and what you found when the trunk was finally opened.

Vocabulary in Action

The Hatfields and the McCoys endured one of the worst **feuds** in American history. The feud between the two warring families occurred from 1878 to 1891 along the Tug Fork River in the West Virginia-Kentucky backcountry. Most of the McCoy family lived on the Kentucky side of the river, while the Hatfields lived mostly on the West Virginia side. Through the course of the feud, several brutal acts—including murder—were committed by members of both families. Many believe the rivalry began when a member of the Hatfield family married a McCoy.

FUN WITH WORDS

Unscramble the letters to form vocabulary words from this chapter. Write the word on the line. Then use the word in a sentence.

1. elabinboam   _____abominable_____

   _____Answers will vary._____

2. citilli   _____illicit_____

   _____.

3. ceategrong   _____congregate_____

   _____.

4. lahette   _____athlete_____

   _____.

5. nosepliox   _____explosion_____

   _____.

6. naglos   _____slogan_____

   _____.

7. laeiroc   _____calorie_____

   _____.

8. learve   _____reveal_____

   _____.

9. bratvei   _____vibrate_____

   _____.

10. esevilu   _____elusive_____

    _____.

Chapter 1   Level F

CHAPTER 2

WORD LIST

Read each word using the pronunciation key.

abstain (ab stān´)
annex (an´ eks)
candidate (kan´ də dāt)
commit (kə mit´)
consequence (kon´ sə kwens)
constellation (kon stə lā´ shən)
depict (di pikt´)
discontent (dis kən tent´)
emigrate (em´ i grāt)
fierce (fērs)
grovel (grov´ əl)
impact (im´ pakt)
juvenile (jōō və nīl)
misfit (mis´ fit)
perch (pərch)
qualm (kwäm)
smolder (smōl´ dər)
tedious (tē´ dē əs)
tension (ten´ shən)
vital (vīt´ əl)

WORD STUDY

Prefixes

The prefix *dis-* means "not" or "the absence of."

disadvantage (dis əd van´ tij) *(n.)* lack of advantage
disagree (dis ə grē´) *(v.)* to not agree
discomfort (dis kum´ fərt) *(n.)* lack of comfort
discontinue (dis kən tin´ yü) *(v.)* to stop; to not continue
disgrace (dis grās´) *(n.)* loss of honor
disobey (dis ə bā´) *(v.)* to not conform; to not follow commands

Challenge Words

alliance (ə lī´ əns)
fluster (flus´ tər)
infamous (in´ fə məs)
misdemeanor (mis də mē´ nər)
turmoil (tər´ moil)

Level F

■ **TEACHER TIP:** See page ix for suggestions on how to use this page.

WORDS IN CONTEXT

Read each sentence below to figure out the meaning of the word in **bold**. Use reasoning skills and the remainder of the sentence to help you. Write the meaning of the word on the line.

1. Is Michael going to be a **candidate** in our school election?

   a person who desires to be elected to some office or honor

2. The head-on **impact** crumpled the bumpers and hoods of both cars.

   a collision of one thing against another; a striking

3. Because of a knee injury, Hannah must **abstain** from jogging for one year.

   to do without

4. When did your ancestors **emigrate** from Japan to the United States?

   to move from one's own country to live in another

5. Vultures often **perch** in treetops as they watch for prey.

   to rest or settle in a high place or on an insecure surface

6. The astronomer pointed out the **constellation** of Orion in the night sky.

   a grouping of stars that form a pattern

7. The weather forecaster warned of the hurricane's **fierce** winds.

   intense; wild; furious

8. My four-year-old brother made a beeline to the library's collection of **juvenile** books.

   of or for children

9. It's hard to choose when I have **qualms** about both summer camps.

   an uneasiness or doubt

10. Is it wise to let the campfire **smolder** after we've gone to bed?

    to burn and smoke without flame

WORD MEANINGS

Word Learning

Study the spelling, part(s) of speech, and meaning(s) of each word. Complete each sentence by writing the word on the line. Then read the sentence.

1. **abstain** *(v.)* to do without

   The doctor told Haley to _____abstain_____ from all dairy products until she feels better.

2. **annex** *(n.)* 1. a part that is added; 2. an added part to a building

   Mr. Lee's office is located next door, in our building's new _____annex_____.

3. **candidate** *(n.)* a person who desires to be elected to some office or honor

   The presidential _____candidate_____ will visit our school before the election.

4. **commit** *(v.)* 1. to involve or pledge oneself; 2. to be bound to do

   The project leader wanted to hire only people who could _____commit_____ to the full two weeks.

5. **consequence** *(n.)* a result of one's actions

   As a _____consequence_____ of spending all day indoors, we missed the lovely weather.

6. **constellation** *(n.)* a grouping of stars that form a pattern

   Luke can name all the stars in his favorite _____constellation_____.

7. **depict** *(v.)* to portray by picture or word

   The artist found a way to _____depict_____ honesty and grace in the portrait of Makayla.

8. **discontent** *(adj.)* 1. unhappy; 2. displeased; 3. dissatisfied; *(n.)* unhappiness or dissatisfaction

   The workers were _____discontent_____ with their low wages.

   The _____discontent_____ of the workers could lead to a bitter strike.

9. **emigrate** *(v.)* to move from one's own country to live in another

   Who will be the next to _____emigrate_____ from Russia to Turkey?

10. **fierce** *(adj.)* 1. intense; 2. wild; 3. furious

    The _____fierce_____ look of the lionfish scares away predators.

11. **grovel** *(v.)* 1. to creep at someone's feet; 2. to humble oneself

Maxwell and Zoe _____grovel_____ when they want more allowance money from their parents.

12. **impact** *(n.)* 1. a collision of one thing against another; 2. a striking

The _____impact_____ of the huge tree hitting the ground shook the entire forest.

13. **juvenile** *(n.)* a young person; *(adj.)* of or for children

Here is a book about travel suitable for a _____juvenile_____ to read.

Playing practical jokes is _____juvenile_____ behavior.

14. **misfit** *(n.)* a person who is not suited for a particular job or group

Being all thumbs, I was a _____misfit_____ in wood shop class.

15. **perch** *(v.)* to rest or settle in a high place or on an insecure surface

With our binoculars we watched an eagle swoop in and _____perch_____ in a tall tree.

16. **qualm** *(n.)* a sudden uneasiness or doubtfulness of the mind

Nicolas has no _____qualm_____ about asking for help when he needs it.

17. **smolder** *(v.)* to burn and smoke without flame

You can put the fire out now or allow it to _____smolder_____ for a while.

18. **tedious** *(adj.)* 1. boring; 2. tiring

Riley took over the _____tedious_____ job of sewing on each button.

19. **tension** *(n.)* 1. the stress that results from stretching; 2. a strain

The sail went up as we increased the _____tension_____ on the ropes.

20. **vital** *(adj.)* 1. essential; 2. critical

Abby's leadership and good sense make her a _____vital_____ part of our team.

Notable Quotes

"The ability to think straight, some knowledge of the past, some vision of the future, some urge to fit that service into the well-being of the community—these are the most **vital** things that education must try to produce."

—Virginia Gildersleeve (1877–1965), academic, U.S. delegate to United Nations Charter Conference

Use Your Vocabulary

Choose the word from the Word List that best completes each sentence. Write the word on the line. You may use the plural form of nouns and the past tense of verbs if necessary.

Our neighbors __1__ to the United States from another country. They were __2__ with the living conditions in their native country and were __3__ in their determination to find a better life. Even today, they tell stories that __4__ how difficult life in their country was. They remember that if homes caught on fire, families could only watch the remains __5__ because often there was no water. Armed soldiers would __6__ on rooftops just to show who was in control. Citizens had to __7__ from criticizing their government, or they would face harsh __8__ . Political __9__ caused neighbors to quarrel and accuse each other.

The long and __10__ process to get permission to leave could take years. Sometimes the only way to get permission was to __11__ and beg. Volunteers __12__ much of their time to help families become __13__ for emigration. Those who wanted to leave would first live with several other people in a small __14__ attached to the village church.

Even after our neighbors received permission to emigrate, they had __15__ about their decision. It was hard to leave family and friends behind. They were comforted by gazing at the stars in the night sky, knowing they would see the same __16__ in their new country. When it came time to leave, each person could only pack a few __17__ items. The __18__ of two ways of life colliding made it difficult for our neighbors to adjust at first. Sometimes they felt like __19__ because they didn't speak English. The elderly members of the family had the most difficulty getting used to things, but the __20__ members felt at home in just a few months.

1. _____ emigrated _____
2. _____ discontent _____
3. _____ fierce _____
4. _____ depict _____
5. _____ smolder _____
6. _____ perch _____
7. _____ abstain _____
8. _____ consequences _____
9. _____ tensions _____
10. _____ tedious _____
11. _____ grovel _____
12. _____ committed _____
13. _____ candidates _____
14. _____ annex _____
15. _____ qualms _____
16. _____ constellations _____
17. _____ vital _____
18. _____ impact _____
19. _____ misfits _____
20. _____ juvenile _____

SYNONYMS

Synonyms are words that have the same or nearly the same meanings.

Part 1 Choose the word from the box that is the best synonym for each group of words. Write the word on the line.

fierce	abstain	discontent	consequence
commit	vital	qualm	tedious

1. untamed, cruel, extreme   _____fierce_____

2. bind, obligate   _____commit_____

3. dull, humdrum, uninteresting   _____tedious_____

4. avoid, give up, not use   _____abstain_____

5. important, necessary, required   _____vital_____

6. outcome, effect, product   _____consequence_____

7. worry, misgiving, dread   _____qualm_____

8. sadness, restlessness; troubled   _____discontent_____

Part 2 Replace the underlined word with a word from the box that means the same or almost the same. Write your answer on the line.

perch	impact	depict	juvenile
annex	emigrate	tension	

9. The expansion will house 16 new offices for extra staff members.

     _____annex_____

10. There's a ledge in the henhouse where the hens can roost. _____perch_____

11. A promise of a better life causes many families to relocate to new places.

     _____emigrate_____

12. The smashing of the logs at the bottom of the slide sent up a big spray of water.

     _____impact_____

13. How would you characterize Martina's skill on the soccer field?

_____ depict _____

14. Kids in trouble appear in youth court. _____ juvenile _____

15. You need to increase the tightness on the strings to tune your guitar.

_____ tension _____

ANTONYMS

Antonyms are words that have opposite or nearly opposite meanings.

Part 1 Choose the word from the box that is the best antonym for each group of words. Write the word on the line.

fierce	abstain	qualm
misfit	tension	juvenile

1. older person; relating to adults _____ juvenile _____

2. person who is accepted _____ misfit _____

3. calm, meek, mild, tame _____ fierce _____

4. take part in something _____ abstain _____

5. lack of stress, relaxation _____ tension _____

6. lack of doubt, security _____ qualm _____

Part 2 Replace the underlined word(s) with a word from the box that means the opposite or almost the opposite. Write your answer on the line.

smolder	discontent	emigrate	vital	tedious

7. The political troubles influenced the man's decision to stay in one place.

_____ emigrate _____

8. The diplomat was unaware that he presented useless information.

_____ vital _____

9. Don't you agree that the TV show on the life cycle of the aphid is <u>interesting</u>?
_____tedious_____

10. The paper in the wastebasket began to <u>blaze</u>. _____smolder_____

11. The bright color of these walls adds to my <u>pleasure</u>. _____discontent_____

 ## WORD STUDY

Prefixes Write the word from the box that has the prefix *dis-* and the same meaning as the next word(s) that follow.

disobey	disagree	discomfort
disadvantage	disgrace	discontinue

1. dis + favorable _____disadvantage_____

2. dis + get along _____disagree_____

3. dis + do as told _____disobey_____

4. dis + freedom from strain _____discomfort_____

5. dis + go on with _____discontinue_____

6. dis + charm _____disgrace_____

Vocabulary in Action

As with many words beginning with *dis-*, one can determine the meaning of ***discontent*** by thinking about the opposite of the word that follows the prefix. Since the word *content* means "satisfied" or "happy," it makes sense that *discontent* means "unhappy."

CHALLENGE WORDS

Word Learning—Challenge!

Study the spelling, part of speech, and meaning of each word. Complete each sentence by writing the word on the line. Then read the sentence.

1. **alliance** *(n.)* bond or connection between countries, parties, or persons

   Kyra and Adrianna formed an _____alliance_____ to beat Marissa in the game.

2. **fluster** *(v.)* to make very confused and bothered

   Driving and parking a car _____fluster_____ Drake so much that he takes the train.

3. **infamous** *(adj.)* having a bad reputation

   The _____infamous_____ outlaw Elena James is not welcome in this town.

4. **misdemeanor** *(n.)* less serious crime than a felony

   Parking illegally is a _____misdemeanor_____, while kidnapping is a felony.

5. **turmoil** *(n.)* the condition of extreme confusion or agitation

   The swarm of angry bees caused a great _____turmoil_____ at the picnic.

Use Your Vocabulary—Challenge!

A Strange Planet You are a space traveler. You and your crew have just landed on a planet inhabited by people whose language and customs are strange to you. On a separate sheet of paper, write a diary entry describing your first day on this planet. Use the Challenge Words above. Describe the landscape and people. Tell about any difficulties you encountered.

Vocabulary in Action

The word *emigrate* is often confused with its homophone— *immigrate. Emigrate* means "to leave one's place of residency and live in another place." For example: She emigrated from Canada to the United States. The word *immigrate,* on the other hand, means "to enter a new a place and become established there." For example: She immigrated to the United States from Canada in 1917.

It is the year 2029. Your pen pal Malpropo, who lives on Excellon 12, has sent you a message on the interspace network. Malpropo's English is not perfect, so you need to figure out the message in a few places. Cross out the words that are incorrect and replace them with the correct vocabulary words from this chapter.

Greetings, friend!

      I have great news. Last week I discovered a new *constellation* ~~conversation~~ of 13 stars. I wish I could *depict* ~~depress~~ for you

the way it looks in our sky. I'm so happy now. I feel that all my bad feelings of *discontent* ~~discount~~ are gone. I no longer think of myself as a *misfit* ~~mister~~ in my group. In fact, Darnag told me I am a *vital* ~~vitamin~~ part of the project. I have decided not to *emigrate* ~~emerald~~ to Excellon 13, but I would like to visit you on

Earth. Write soon.

                         Your friend,

                         Malpropo

WORD LIST

Read each word using the pronunciation key.

accelerate (ak sel´ ə rāt)
captivity (kap tiv´ ə tē)
conserve (kən sərv´)
despair (di spâr´)
disguise (dis gīz´)
enamel (i nam´ əl)
exotic (eg zot´ ic)
figurative (fig´ yər ə tiv)
gruesome (grōō´ səm)
implement (im´ plə mənt)
keen (kēn)
mismanage (mis man´ ij)
notation (nō tā´ shən)
perishable (per´ i shə bəl)
procedure (pro sē´ jər)
quench (kwench)
savage (sav´ ij)
sneer (snēr)
terminal (tər´ mə nəl)
vocation (vō cā´ shən)

WORD STUDY

Homophones

Homophones are words that have the same pronunciation but different meanings.

chili (chil´ ē) *(n.)* a hot-tasting pod of red pepper
chilly (chil´ ē) *(adj.)* unpleasantly cool

canvas (kan´ vəs) *(n.)* firmly woven cloth usually of cotton or linen
canvass (kan´ vəs) *(v.)* 1. to examine in detail; 2 to go to an area to try and get votes for a candidate

overseas (ō vər sēz´) *(adv.)* across the sea
oversees (ō vər sēz´) *(v.)* supervises

Challenge Words

amiss (ə mis´)
dissuade (di swād´)
futile (fyōō´ təl)
meager (mē´ gər)
prudent (prōōd´ ənt)

■ **TEACHER TIP:** See page ix for suggestions on how to use this page.

WORDS IN CONTEXT

Read each sentence below to figure out the meaning of the word in **bold**. Use reasoning skills and the remainder of the sentence to help you. Write the meaning of the word on the line.

1. We need to establish a **procedure** for ending our club meetings.

   plan; a way of doing something

2. Please put the **perishable** food in the refrigerator so it won't spoil.

   capable of decaying; biodegradable; decomposable

3. A tall glass of cold lemonade can **quench** your thirst on a hot day.

   to satisfy

4. Farm **implements**, including tractors and plows, will be sold at the auction.

   tools

5. Because of the drought, Matthew wants us to **conserve** water.

   to preserve; to keep from being used up

6. What clever **disguise** will Alexis wear to the costume party?

   a mask or cover up

7. The **gruesome** lizardlike creature in the movie disgusted me.

   hideous

8. Alexandra was in **despair** over the loss of her grandmother's ring.

   hopelessness; discouragement

9. I am careful not to **mismanage** my savings so that I'll have money when I need it.

   to handle poorly

10. To someone raised in a rural town, the food in Thailand might seem **exotic**.

    strange; foreign; unknown

WORD MEANINGS

Word Learning

Study the spelling, part(s) of speech, and meaning(s) of each word. Complete each sentence by writing the word on the line. Then read the sentence.

1. **accelerate** *(v.)* to increase speed

    The minivan needed to _____accelerate_____ to pass the truck on the highway.

2. **captivity** *(n.)* the condition of being held against one's will

    Many zoos use natural settings instead of caged _____captivity_____.

3. **conserve** *(v.)* 1. to preserve; 2. to keep from being used up

    Recycling is one way to _____conserve_____ Earth's natural resources.

4. **despair** *(n.)* 1. hopelessness; 2. discouragement; *(v.)* to lose all faith or hope

    The assassination of the president left the country in _____despair_____.

    Don't _____despair_____; the football game isn't over yet.

5. **disguise** *(n.)* a mask or cover up; *(v.)* to mask or conceal one's appearance so as to look like someone else

    Kaitlyn needs a clever _____disguise_____ so that no one will recognize her.

    Thomas will _____disguise_____ himself as a clown.

6. **enamel** *(n.)* a surface or outer covering that has a smooth, glossy appearance; *(v.)* to cover or decorate with a smooth, glossy covering

    This toothpaste will help to whiten the _____enamel_____ of your teeth.

    Devin showed us how to _____enamel_____ our clay pots.

7. **exotic** *(adj.)* 1. strange; 2. foreign; 3. unknown

    The newly retired couple was ready for a trip to an _____exotic_____ place.

8. **figurative** *(adj.)* using words or phrases to mean something different than their usual meaning

    To say that the snow is a quilt over the fields is a _____figurative_____ description.

9. **gruesome** *(adj.)* 1. hideous; 2. causing terror or fear

    A _____gruesome_____ main character might ensure the movie's success.

10. **implement** *(n.)* a tool, an instrument, or an utensil

    The dentist used an _____implement_____ that looked like a hook.

11. **keen** *(adj.)* quick; sharp; enthusiastic

Quiz show contestants are rewarded for their _____keen_____ minds.

12. **mismanage** *(v.)* to control or handle poorly

Mark can buy a snowboard if he doesn't _____mismanage_____ his money.

13. **notation** *(n.)* a brief written record

You'll find the source of the _____notation_____ at the end of the book.

14. **perishable** *(adj.)* 1. capable of decaying; 2. biodegradable; 3. decomposable

The _____perishable_____ foods will be shipped in a refrigerated truck.

15. **procedure** *(n.)* 1. plan; 2. a way of doing something

Please read the _____procedure_____ for emergencies.

16. **quench** *(v.)* 1. to satisfy; 2. to put out or extinguish

Paige used baking soda to _____quench_____ the grease fire on the stove.

17. **savage** *(adj.)* 1. fierce; 2. wild; 3. cruel

Eli likes animal movies that create lovable characters from _____savage_____ beasts.

18. **sneer** *(n.)* a look or words that express scorn; *(v.)* 1. to show scorn by looks or words; 2. to taunt

The young, rebellious actor was a master of the _____sneer_____.

The referee considers it unsportsmanlike when players _____sneer_____ at rivals.

19. **terminal** *(n.)* 1. the end; 2. end part; 3. a freight or passenger train station; *(adj.)* 1. fatal; 2. deadly

Molly departed the train at the _____terminal_____.

Before the discovery of penicillin, strep throat was sometimes _____terminal_____.

20. **vocation** *(n.)* a person's occupation or business.

Leah felt her _____vocation_____ was to manage a homeless shelter.

Use Your Vocabulary

Choose the word from the Word List that best completes each sentence. Write the word on the line. You may use the plural form of nouns and the past tense of verbs if necessary.

My cousin's chosen __1__ is working as a conservationist in Africa. He keeps a journal of scientific __2__ about the animals he sees. He also records each day's __3__ in order to improve the way he observes animals. In addition, he composes poetry and uses beautiful __4__ language to describe the beauty of the land around him.

The tan safari clothes he wears help __5__ him so that the animals don't notice him. He got too close to a rhinoceros once and had to __6__ his vehicle to escape. He narrowly saved himself from a(n) __7__, gory end. Not all animals are __8__ beasts, though. Many are just curious, like the monkeys who stole his utensils and cooking __9__. He's certain that the sassy monkeys __10__ as they made off with his glossy, new __11__ pots and pans.

Life in central Africa is difficult but not __12__. It's important to not __13__ your food. You don't want to run out, and you don't want __14__ food to spoil. Also, you must carry clean water to __15__ your thirst after a long hike.

My cousin cannot stand to see animals held in __16__, yet he feels __17__ for the disappearance of many species. So he works hard to __18__ the animals' territory and protect their freedom.

I have a(n) __19__ interest in going to Africa to visit my cousin. There's nothing I'd rather do. In fact, I would go tomorrow because I am ready to have an unusual, __20__ adventure.

1. _____ vocation _____

2. _____ notations _____

3. _____ procedure _____

4. _____ figurative _____

5. _____ disguise _____

6. _____ accelerate _____

7. _____ gruesome _____

8. _____ savage _____

9. _____ implements _____

10. _____ sneered _____

11. _____ enamel _____

12. _____ terminal _____

13. _____ mismanage _____

14. _____ perishable _____

15. _____ quench _____

16. _____ captivity _____

17. _____ despair _____

18. _____ conserve _____

19. _____ keen _____

20. _____ exotic _____

SYNONYMS

Synonyms are words that have the same or nearly the same meanings.

Part 1 Choose the word from the box that is the best synonym for each group of words. Write the word on the line.

disguise	notation	conserve	implement
gruesome	accelerate	captivity	vocation

1. job, craft, career _____vocation_____

2. costume; hide, obscure _____disguise_____

3. comment, message, writing _____notation_____

4. hurry, advance, go faster _____accelerate_____

5. protect, save, guard _____conserve_____

6. frightful, grim, scary _____gruesome_____

7. lack of freedom, imprisonment _____captivity_____

8. piece of equipment _____implement_____

Part 2 Replace the underlined word(s) with a word from the box that means the same or almost the same. Write your answer on the line.

keen	manage	procedure	sneer
quench	despair	savage	

9. "Get that <u>scornful look</u> off your face," the police officer said to the thief.
   _____sneer_____

10. Edward showed a <u>spirited</u> interest in learning rock climbing.
    _____keen_____

11. The tigers in the circus act were once <u>ferocious</u> beasts.
    _____savage_____

12. The ushers need to keep control and not <u>mess up</u> the crowd.
    _____mismanage_____

13. The surgeon developed his own <u>program</u> for removing kidneys.

procedure

14. The new teacher is the first to <u>fulfill</u> Erik's thirst for knowledge.

quench

15. The beginning of the school year may be difficult, but don't <u>feel hopeless</u>.

despair

ANTONYMS

Antonyms are words that have opposite or nearly opposite meanings.

Part 1 Choose the word from the box that is the best antonym for each group of words. Write the word on the line.

captivity	mismanage	perishable	savage	conserve

1. waste, destroy, throw away

conserve

2. take care of properly

mismanage

3. freedom, independence, liberty

captivity

4. tamed, gentle, kind

savage

5. lasting, not easily spoiled

perishable

Vocabulary in Action

Theodore Roosevelt was the 26th President of the United States. He was known for his determination, stubbornness, and grit. Roosevelt also had a deep love for the natural world. His love of nature and wildlife inspired him to help **conserve** land and create national parks. While he was president, he created 51 national parks, four big-game refuges, and the first national game reserve. Roosevelt also added 43 million acres of national forest.

Part 2 Replace the underlined word(s) with a word from the box that means the opposite or almost the opposite. Write your answer on the line.

accelerate   gruesome   keen   terminal   exotic

6. Scott's comments reveal the extent of his <u>dull</u> wit. _____ keen _____

7. I think this room needs an <u>ordinary</u> rug to go with this wallpaper.
   _____ exotic _____

8. Time seems to <u>slow down</u> as the clock nears 3:00 p.m. _____ accelerate _____

9. At the particularly <u>pleasing</u> part of the play, several people walked out.
   _____ gruesome _____

10. You'll find your luggage at the <u>starting point</u>. _____ terminal _____

WORD STUDY

Homonyms Choose the homonym that correctly completes each sentence. Write the word on the line.

1. We'll cook up a big pot of (chilly, chili) for the soccer fans.
   _____ chili _____

2. The shirt you are wearing is very thick; it must be made of (canvass, canvas).
   _____ canvas _____

3. The unseasonably (chilly, chili) weather might discourage visitors.
   _____ chilly _____

4. The Language Club will go (overseas, oversees) to study French for three weeks.
   _____ overseas _____

5. I am going to (canvass, canvas) the hallways looking for my lost locker key.
   _____ canvass _____

6. Who (overseas, oversees) the cafeteria at lunchtime? _____ oversees _____

CHALLENGE WORDS

Word Learning—Challenge!

Study the spelling, part of speech, and meaning(s) of each word. Complete each sentence by writing the word on the line. Then read the sentence.

1. **amiss** *(adj.)* 1. not in the right order; 2. out of place

   I knew something was _____ amiss _____ when I saw the broken dish on the floor.

2. **dissuade** *(v.)* to advise against something

   Adriana tried to _____ dissuade _____ them against driving on the icy road.

3. **futile** *(adj.)* 1. not producing; 2. vain; 3. useless

   Drew made one more _____ futile _____ attempt and then gave up.

4. **meager** *(adj.)* deficient in quality or strength

   A soccer team with only four players is _____ meager _____ in numbers.

5. **prudent** *(adj.)* marked by great wisdom or good judgment

   A _____ prudent _____ person always carries an umbrella on rainy days.

Use Your Vocabulary—Challenge!

Save the Cat A cat is caught up high in a tree. It is your job to help the cat find its way to safety. On a separate sheet of paper, write an explanation of how you would rescue the cat from the tree. Use the Challenge Words above. Be sure to describe the situation and tell how you would go about solving the problem.

Notable Quotes

"When I **despair**, I remember that all through history the ways of truth and love have always won. There have been tyrants, and murderers, and for a time they can seem invincible, but in the end they always fall. Think of it—always."

—Mohondas "Mahatma" Gandhi (1869–1948), peace activist, political and spiritual leader of India

FUN WITH WORDS

The clues and some letters from this puzzle are missing! Fill in the missing letters of the vocabulary words from this chapter in the puzzle. Then write a clue for each word.

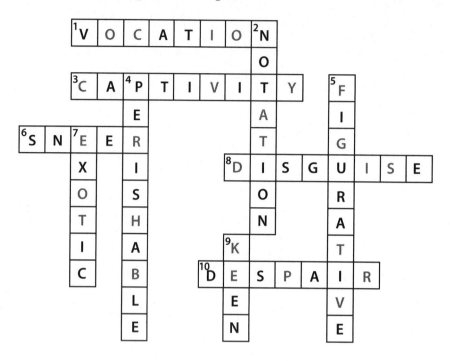

Across

1. a person's occupation or business _____

3. the condition of being held against one's will _____

6. a look or words that express scorn _____

8. a mask or cover-up _____

10. hopelessness; discouragement _____

Down

2. a brief, written record _____

4. capable of decaying; biodegradable; decomposable _____

5. using words or phrases to mean something different than their usual meaning _____

7. strange; foreign; unknown _____

9. quick; sharp; enthusiastic _____

Chapter 3   Level F

Review 1–3

Word Meanings Fill in the bubble of the word that is best defined by each phrase.

1. to stop oneself from doing something
   - (a.) denounce
   - (b.) accelerate
   - (c.) despair
   - **(d.) abstain**

2. the state of being locked up
   - **(a.) captivity**
   - (b.) annex
   - (c.) consequence
   - (d.) vocation

3. not allowed by law
   - (a.) abominable
   - **(b.) illicit**
   - (c.) juvenile
   - (d.) judicious

4. long and dull
   - (a.) elusive
   - (b.) mischievous
   - (c.) exotic
   - **(d.) tedious**

5. making good decisions
   - (a.) figurative
   - (b.) vital
   - **(c.) judicious**
   - (d.) gruesome

6. to protect
   - (a.) mismanage
   - (b.) commit
   - **(c.) conserve**
   - (d.) disguise

7. to make something known
   - **(a.) reveal**
   - (b.) grovel
   - (c.) emigrate
   - (d.) denounce

8. the way something is done
   - (a.) notation
   - **(b.) procedure**
   - (c.) vocation
   - (d.) constellation

9. violently cruel and wild
   - (a.) juvenile
   - (b.) elusive
   - **(c.) fierce**
   - (d.) exotic

10. to make a charge against
    - **(a.) denounce**
    - (b.) disguise
    - (c.) grovel
    - (d.) abstain

11. to go faster
    - (a.) vibrate
    - **(b.) accelerate**
    - (c.) congregate
    - (d.) emigrate

12. horrible and scary
    - (a.) elusive
    - (b.) tedious
    - (c.) figurative
    - **(d.) gruesome**

13. to describe in words or images
    - (a.) smolder
    - **(b.) depict**
    - (c.) emigrate
    - (d.) sneer

14. the effect of a cause
    - (a.) qualm
    - (b.) explosion
    - **(c.) consequence**
    - (d.) calorie

15. a fight or an argument that lasts a long time
    - (a.) terminal
    - (b.) notation
    - **(c.) feud**
    - (d.) tendon

16. to gather together as a group
    - **(a.) congregate**
    - (b.) vibrate
    - (c.) commit
    - (d.) conserve

17. a person's line of work
  (a.) captivity   **(b.) vocation**   (c.) procedure   (d.) impact

18. absolutely necessary
  (a.) perishable   (b.) figurative   (c.) judicious   **(d.) vital**

19. to make a mess of
  (a.) mismanage   (b.) denounce   (c.) accelerate   (d.) abstain

20. a person running for office
  (a.) qualm   (b.) constellation   (c.) athlete   **(d.) candidate**

Sentence Completion
Choose the word from the box that best completes each of the following sentences. Write the word in the blank.

keen	emigrated	mischievous	annex	misfit
abominable	discontent	perishable	athlete	slogan

1. Casey is a(n) _____mischievous_____ boy who loves to play tricks on people.

2. Have you visited the beautiful new _____annex_____ to the public library yet?

3. I try to keep my mind _____keen_____ by solving one chess puzzle every morning.

4. After we moved, my sister seemed _____discontent_____ until she got used to our new home.

5. I heard that the new _____slogan_____ is "Yes we can! Go visit Michigan!"

6. The food bank only accepts items that are not _____perishable_____ and do not have to be refrigerated.

7. The star _____athlete_____ on our track team hurt her leg yesterday.

8. Our family _____emigrated_____ from France many years ago.

9. Cruelty to animals is _____abominable_____ behavior for any person.

10. Calvin felt like a(n) _____misfit_____ because he was the only one who didn't like the music.

Fill in the Blanks
Fill in the bubble of the pair of words that best completes each sentence.

1. The 50-year _____ between the families was caused by the Miller's _____ in the neighborhood ghost.
   a. disguise, tension
   b. feud, disbelief
   c. candidate, vocation
   d. grovel, notation

2. If you do not _____ from eating junk food, you will feel the _____.
   a. denounce, parody
   b. conserve, notation
   c. abstain, consequences
   d. reveal, tension

3. If you plan to _____ to being in the play, it is _____ that you rehearse your lines before rehearsal.
   a. commit, vital
   b. depict, perishable
   c. mismanage, elusive
   d. emigrate, keen

4. After hearing the two _____ running for class president debate, I decided that Derrick was far more _____ than Chad.
   a. juveniles, terminal
   b. candidates, keen
   c. calories, judicious
   d. slogans, mischievous

5. The novel's main character was a(n) _____ villain whose bloody, _____ deeds horrified the whole city.
   a. abominable, discontent
   b. exotic, juvenile
   c. savage, gruesome
   d. tedious, perishable

6. The surgical _____ is difficult and _____.
   a. parody, perishable
   b. explosion, vital
   c. procedure, tedious
   d. captivity, terminal

7. For the pet show, we _____ our llama as the _____ snowman.
   a. denounced, illicit
   b. sneered, fierce
   c. emigrated, gruesome
   d. disguised, abominable

8. The judge's words had a(n) _____ on the _____ offenders.
   a. impact, juvenile
   b. explosion, fierce
   c. vocation, keen
   d. disbelief, mischievous

9. The _____ fans yelled out their _____ each time their idol scored a goal.
   a. savage's, parody
   b. athlete's, slogan
   c. constellation's, disbelief
   d. misfit's, implement

10. A(n) _____ person will never _____ a crime.
    a. illicit, vibrate
    b. savage, smolder
    c. judicious, commit
    d. enamel, mismanage

Classifying Words
Sort the words in the box by writing each word to complete a phrase in the correct category.

accelerate	calories	congregated	consequences	constellation
disbelief	disguise	elusive	explosion	feud
fierce	illicit	juvenile	mischievous	mismanage
notation	perched	procedures	tension	vital

Words You Might Hear in Court

1. recognize the criminal's clever _____disguise_____
2. commit a(n) _____illicit_____ act
3. the _____consequences_____ of your actions
4. the jurors' _____disbelief_____ of the witness's story
5. a young _____juvenile_____ offender's only crime

Words You Might Hear at the Zoo

6. the _____mischievous_____ monkey's pranks
7. a(n) _____fierce_____ beast's frightening roar
8. a parrot _____perched_____ on a branch
9. a crowd _____congregated_____ around an exhibit
10. the nervous _____tension_____ between the two male lions

Words You Might Hear in an Office

11. make a(n) _____notation_____ in the file
12. follow all office _____procedures_____
13. a long-standing _____feud_____ between the two departments
14. try not to _____mismanage_____ the project
15. figure out how to _____accelerate_____ the schedule

Words You Might Hear in a Science Laboratory

16. the boom of a chemical _____explosion_____
17. looking at a(n) _____constellation_____ through a telescope
18. record _____vital_____ information in a log
19. analyzing the number of _____calories_____ in food
20. pin down a(n) _____elusive_____ idea

WORD LIST

Read each word using the pronunciation key.

acute (ə kyo͞ot´)

appreciative (ə prē´ shə tiv)

cavity (kav´ ə tē)

consider (kən sid´ ər)

crystal (kris´ təl)

despise (di spīz´)

displace (dis plās´)

enforcement (in fôrs´ mənt)

flex (fleks)

gulf (gulf)

incomprehensible (in kom pri hen´ sə bəl)

legislate (lej´ is lāt)

nobility (nō bil´ i tē)

physical (fiz´ i kəl)

radiant (rā´ dē ənt)

scant (skant)

sheen (shēn)

solitary (sol´ i târ ē)

trifle (trī´ fəl)

volume (vol´ yo͞om)

WORD STUDY

Suffixes

The suffix *-hood* means "a condition of" or "a group of."

adulthood (ə dult´ ho͝od) *(n.)* the condition of being an adult

childhood (chīld´ ho͝od) *(n.)* the condition of being a child

falsehood (fôls´ ho͝od) *(n.)* an untrue statement; a lie

livelihood (līv´ lē ho͝od) *(n.)* a means of living; a way to support

motherhood (mə´ thər ho͝od) *(n.)* the condition of being a mother

neighborhood (nā´ bər ho͝od) *(n.)* people living near one another

Challenge Words

anonymous (ə nä´ nə məs)

dishearten (dis här´ tən)

eradicate (i ra´ də kāt)

insinuate (in sin´ yə wāt)

prescribe (pri skrīb´)

41

Level F

■ **TEACHER TIP:** See page ix for suggestions on how to use this page.

WORDS IN CONTEXT

Read each sentence below to figure out the meaning of the word in **bold**. Use reasoning skills and the remainder of the sentence to help you. Write the meaning of the word on the line.

1. Your words are **incomprehensible** when you talk too quickly.

   not understandable

2. Wrestling takes great strength and is a very **physical** sport.

   of or relating to the body

3. I **despise** cooked spinach, but I like raw spinach in a fresh salad.

   to dislike strongly

4. Joshua likes to take **solitary** walks along the empty beach near his home.

   single; isolated; lonely

5. The officer's duty is to see to the **enforcement** of laws and to arrest offenders.

   a forcing to obey

6. Thank-you notes are a way to let others know that you are **appreciative** of their gifts.

   having or showing gratitude

7. Sarah has a **cavity** in her tooth that the dentist needs to fill.

   a hole

8. Take some time to **consider** each choice of dessert.

   to think carefully about something before making a decision

9. The duke and his cousin, the earl, come from a long family line of **nobility**.

   people who are of high rank, title, or birth

10. The **radiant** glow from the fireplace warmed and cheered the room.

    bright; shining

WORD MEANINGS

Word Learning

Study the spelling, part(s) of speech, and meaning(s) of each word. Complete each sentence by writing the word on the line. Then read the sentence.

1. **acute** *(adj.)* 1. sharp; 2. keen, quick, intelligent

   Nathan hit the ground, felt an _____ **acute** _____ stab of pain, and knew his arm was broken.

2. **appreciative** *(adj.)* 1. having or showing gratitude; 2. recognizing the value of someone or something

   An actor's reward is the applause of an _____ **appreciative** _____ audience.

3. **cavity** *(n.)* 1. a vacant space; 2. a hole

   Before cooking the turkey, fill the abdominal _____ **cavity** _____ with stuffing.

4. **consider** *(v.)* to think carefully about something before making a decision

   Listen to the question and _____ **consider** _____ your answer before speaking.

5. **crystal** *(n.)* a colorless, transparent rock or glass; *(adj.)* 1. clear; 2. able to be seen through

   How long does it take to clean each _____ **crystal** _____ on the chandelier?

   Cameron could see beautiful fish in the _____ **crystal** _____ clear water.

6. **despise** *(v.)* to dislike strongly

   I enjoy cooking, but I _____ **despise** _____ washing all the dishes after the meal.

7. **displace** *(v.)* to replace or take the place of

   Will hip-hop music ever _____ **displace** _____ rock music on this radio station?

8. **enforcement** *(n.)* a forcing to obey

   Police found that _____ **enforcement** _____ of the new speed limit kept them busy.

9. **flex** *(v.)* 1. to bend or move; 2. to move the muscles by contraction

   Come on now; _____ **flex** _____ your arm so I can see your muscles.

10. **gulf** *(n.)* 1. a large section of an ocean or sea that has land around most of it; 2. a wide gap

    Kevin will follow the west coast of Florida as he sails the _____ **gulf** _____.

11. **incomprehensible** *(adj.)* not understandable

Natalie's speech was not only difficult to hear, it was ___incomprehensible___.

12. **legislate** *(v.)* to make or create laws

Congress ordered each state to ___legislate___ a lower speed limit.

13. **nobility** *(n.)* people who are of high rank, title, or birth

The palace and the royal yacht are only for the use of the ___nobility___.

14. **physical** *(adj.)* of or relating to the body; *(n.)* a medical examination by a physician

Let's get some ___physical___ exercise by running a few football plays.

At my annual ___physical___, the doctor said I'm in great shape.

15. **radiant** *(adj.)* 1. bright; 2. shining; 3. beaming

The winner accepted her trophy with a ___radiant___ smile.

16. **scant** *(adj.)* barely enough in size or quantity

Mariah held up the ___scant___ piece of fabric and decided to make a skirt for her doll.

17. **sheen** *(n.)* 1. a brightness; 2. a glow

The winning goat's coat had a clean, healthy ___sheen___.

18. **solitary** *(adj.)* 1. alone; 2. single; 3. isolated; 4. lonely

Mason enjoyed his ___solitary___ life in a remote mountain cabin.

19. **trifle** *(v.)* 1. to treat someone or something as unimportant; 2. to handle something idly

Do not ___trifle___ with airport security.

20. **volume** *(n.)* 1. the amount of space that something contains or fills; 2. a large amount of something; 3. the degree of loudness

Is the ___volume___ of liquid in the tall glass the same as in the short glass?

> *Vocabulary in Action*
>
> Words that can be made from **legislate** include *legislator,* a noun meaning "one that makes laws"; *legislation,* a noun meaning "the act of legislating"; *legislative,* an adjective; and *legislatively,* an adverb.

Use Your Vocabulary

Choose the word from the Word List that best completes each sentence. Write the word on the line. You may use the plural form of nouns and the past tense of verbs if necessary.

Last weekend I had an attack of loneliness. It all started in 1 education class where my older sister is a gym helper. With my 2 vision, I was able to see the other end of the gym, where the boys were lifting weights. I was watching them 3 their muscles, so I was paying 4 attention when my sister Amy tried to get class started. Usually I 5 Amy my best friend, but sometimes she takes being a gym helper a little too seriously. On Friday, she acted like she didn't care about anything but strict 6 of the rules. She blew her whistle in an insulting way and shouted, "OK, turn down the loud 7 . Line up NOW!"

My friends groaned, and I made a face. "Amy acts like she's some kind of 8 ," I said. "Someone should 9 a law about girls who think they know everything." The minute the words were out I was sorry. Of course, I didn't mean it. Sometimes my behavior is 10 , even to me. Then I looked up, and there was my sister. From the look on her face it was 11 clear that she had heard what I said.

At home after school, I felt like there was a(n) giant 12 between Amy and me. It got worse when I was 13 from our room by the girlfriend she had invited to spend the weekend. I felt worse than the time I had a(n) 14 in my tooth. After a(n) 15 weekend, I was sadder than ever. I wanted to make up, but I didn't know what Amy would say. Finally I went to our room. Amy was brushing her hair. Her hair had a beautiful 16 , but her face looked sad. "I know you 17 me," I began, "but I'm really sorry for what I said. I don't even know why I said it."

My sister's face broke into a(n) glowing, 18 smile. "I'm sorry too," she replied. "I didn't mean to 19 with your feelings."

Sometimes people make mistakes, but friends get over them. My sister and I are friends again. From now on, we'll be more 20 of each other.

1. _____ physical
2. _____ acute
3. _____ flex
4. _____ scant
5. _____ consider
6. _____ enforcement
7. _____ volume
8. _____ nobility
9. _____ legislate
10. _____ incomprehensible
11. _____ crystal
12. _____ gulf
13. _____ displaced
14. _____ cavity
15. _____ solitary
16. _____ sheen
17. _____ despise
18. _____ radiant
19. _____ trifle
20. _____ appreciative

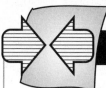

SYNONYMS

Synonyms are words that have the same or nearly the same meanings.

Part 1 Choose the word from the box that is the best synonym for each group of words. Write the word on the line.

despise	sheen	scant	displace
solitary	crystal	legislate	appreciative

1. enact, make laws, pass _____ legislate

2. scarce, insufficient, inadequate _____ scant

3. shine, polish, gloss _____ sheen

4. one, individual, lonesome _____ solitary

5. thankful, grateful, indebted to _____ appreciative

6. hate, scorn, condemn _____ despise

7. transparent, see-through; quartz _____ crystal

8. remove, dislodge, eject _____ displace

Part 2 Replace the underlined word(s) with a word from the box that means the same or almost the same. Write your answer on the line.

gulf	consider	radiant	physical
trifle	incomprehensible	nobility	

9. We flew over a <u>large body of water</u> on our way from Florida to Mexico.
_____ gulf

10. Our walkway was lined with <u>bright</u> candlelight. _____ radiant

11. The veteran ballplayers offhandedly <u>fiddle</u> with their bats. _____ trifle

12. Each camper needs to have a <u>checkup</u> before leaving for camp.
_____ physical

13. I can't read this because Bradley's handwriting is <u>unclear</u>. _____ incomprehensible

14. The shah gave us a sense of <u>royalty</u>. _____ nobility

15. The jury is instructed to <u>think over</u> the testimony of all witnesses carefully.

      consider

 **ANTONYMS**

Antonyms are words that have opposite or nearly opposite meanings.

Part 1 Choose the word from the box that is the best antonym for each group of words. Write the word on the line.

acute	cavity	appreciative	solitary	sheen

1. giving no thanks, not obliged   appreciative

2. dull, dim-witted, slow   acute

3. filled space, solid area   cavity

4. dimness   sheen

5. accompanied, attended, surrounded   solitary

Part 2 Replace the underlined word(s) with a word from the box that means the opposite or almost the opposite. Write your answer on the line.

flex	scant	nobility	despise	incomprehensible

6. There is <u>plenty of</u> food in the pantry to feed this number of people.

     scant

7. The dining cars on the train are reserved for the <u>common people</u>.

    nobility

8. The directions for Julie's new computer were <u>easy to understand</u>.

  incomprehensible

9. Our pythons <u>love</u> the cold weather.   despise

10. To improve your exercise session, <u>relax</u> your muscles frequently.

    flex

WORD STUDY

Suffixes Choose the word from the box that best completes what each person said.

adulthood	livelihood	childhood
falsehood	neighborhood	motherhood

1. A woman: Watching your child leave for the first day of school is a difficult part of _____motherhood_____.

2. Senior citizen: I have been enjoying _____adulthood_____ for a very long time.

3. Courtroom judge: I will not tolerate a single _____falsehood_____ in this trial.

4. Community leader: We will work together to make this _____neighborhood_____ safe.

5. Teenager: I don't want bunk beds anymore. I have left _____childhood_____ behind.

6. Firefighter: I rescue people and put out fires for my _____livelihood_____.

Notable Quotes

"**Childhood** is the fiery furnace in which we are melted down to essentials, and that essential shaped for good."

—Katherine Anne Porter (1890–1980),
writer, novelist, political activist

CHALLENGE WORDS

Word Learning—Challenge!

Study the spelling, part of speech, and meaning(s) of each word. Complete each sentence by writing the word on the line. Then read the sentence.

1. **anonymous** *(adj.)* not identified

   Dillon never did get the name of the _____anonymous_____ caller.

2. **dishearten** *(v.)* to make someone lose motivation or spirit

   The bad weather may _____dishearten_____ the picnickers.

3. **eradicate** *(v.)* to remove completely, as if pulling up by the root

   This weed killer should _____eradicate_____ the dandelions.

4. **insinuate** *(v.)* to communicate or suggest in an indirect way

   Bethany will _____insinuate_____ that you should hurry by pointing to her watch.

5. **prescribe** *(v.)* 1. to designate a plan or guide for; 2. to give a medical prescription

   Doctor Sims will _____prescribe_____ some medicine to reduce your fever.

Use Your Vocabulary—Challenge!

After-School Bizarre Imagine you have planned an educational after-school program for kids under 12 in your school, but something has gone haywire. The children have begun to take control. What can you do? On a separate sheet of paper, write about your experience. Use the Challenge Words above. Be sure to answer the questions *who, what, where, when, why,* and *how.*

> ## Vocabulary in Action
>
> Breaking the word **dishearten** into two sections—prefix and root—is a way to remember its meaning. The Latin prefix *dis-* means "to do the opposite of," and *hearten* means "to encourage." Putting the prefix and root together gets you close to the definition of *dishearten*: "to make someone lose motivation or spirit."

FUN WITH WORDS

Write the word from the Word List that matches each definition. Write one letter of the word in each blank. Then use the numbered letters to answer the riddle.

1. water that has land around three sides   <u>G</u> <u>U</u> <u>L</u> <u>F</u>
                                                        1 2

2. a forcing to obey   <u>E</u> <u>N</u> <u>F</u> <u>O</u> <u>R</u> <u>C</u> <u>E</u> <u>M</u> <u>E</u> <u>N</u> <u>T</u>
                                                      3   4

3. an examination by a doctor   <u>P</u> <u>H</u> <u>Y</u> <u>S</u> <u>I</u> <u>C</u> <u>A</u> <u>L</u>
                                       5

4. barely enough in quantity   <u>S</u> <u>C</u> <u>A</u> <u>N</u> <u>T</u>
                                     6

5. bright and shining   <u>R</u> <u>A</u> <u>D</u> <u>I</u> <u>A</u> <u>N</u> <u>T</u>
                           7

6. a colorless, transparent rock   <u>C</u> <u>R</u> <u>Y</u> <u>S</u> <u>T</u> <u>A</u> <u>L</u>
                               8   9

7. people of noble rank   <u>N</u> <u>O</u> <u>B</u> <u>I</u> <u>L</u> <u>I</u> <u>T</u> <u>Y</u>
                          10   11

8. to take the place of   <u>D</u> <u>I</u> <u>S</u> <u>P</u> <u>L</u> <u>A</u> <u>C</u> <u>E</u>
                             12

9. to handle something idly   <u>T</u> <u>R</u> <u>I</u> <u>F</u> <u>L</u> <u>E</u>
                            13

10. to bend or contract   <u>F</u> <u>L</u> <u>E</u> <u>X</u>
                  14

Which president had the largest family?

<u>G</u> <u>E</u> <u>O</u> <u>R</u> <u>G</u> <u>E</u>   <u>W</u> <u>A</u> <u>S</u> <u>H</u> <u>I</u> <u>N</u> <u>G</u> <u>T</u> <u>O</u> <u>N</u> .
1 3 10 13 1 3   6 12 5 7 4 1 9 10 4

<u>H</u> <u>E</u>   <u>W</u> <u>A</u> <u>S</u>   <u>T</u> <u>H</u> <u>E</u>   <u>F</u> <u>A</u> <u>T</u> <u>H</u> <u>E</u> <u>R</u>
5 3   6 12   9 5 3   14 6 9 5 3 13

<u>O</u> <u>F</u>   <u>O</u> <u>U</u> <u>R</u>   <u>C</u> <u>O</u> <u>U</u> <u>N</u> <u>T</u> <u>R</u> <u>Y</u> .
10 14   10 2 13   8 10 2 4 9 13 11

WORD LIST

Read each word using the pronunciation key.

absorb (ab sôrb´)
adhere (əd hēr´)
associate (*v.* ə sō´ shē āt) (*adj., n.* ə sō´ shē it)
celestial (sə les´ chəl)
contentment (kən tent´ mənt)
destiny (des´ tə nē)
disposable (dis pō´ zə bəl)
engrave (in grāv´)
frantic (fran´ tik)
gullible (gul´ ə bəl)
induce (in do͞os´)
leisure (lē´ zhər)
nomad (nō´ mad)
pedestal (ped´ is təl)
pigment (pig´ mənt)
radioactivity (rā dē ō ak tiv´ ə tē)
scholar (skol´ ər)
sparse (spärs)
triumph (trī´ əmf)
voluntary (vol´ ən târ ē)

WORD STUDY

Root Words

The Latin root word *port* means "to carry."

portable (pôrt´ ə bəl) *(adj.)* easily carried
portfolio (pôrt fō´ lī ō) *(n.)* a case for carrying papers
portage (pôr´ tij) *(v.)* to carry overland
transport (trans´ pôrt) *(n.)* a carrying from one place to another
export (ek spôrt´) *(v.)* to send out of one country
report (ri pôrt´) *(v.)* to give an account of something

Challenge Words

barren (bâr´ ən)
circumscribe (sər´ kəm skrīb)
inconsistent (in kən sis´ tənt)
lavish (lav´ ish)
plight (plīt)

■ **TEACHER TIP:** See page ix for suggestions on how to use this page.

WORDS IN CONTEXT

Read each sentence below to figure out the meaning of the word in **bold**. Use reasoning skills and the remainder of the sentence to help you. Write the meaning of the word on the line.

1. This sponge will **absorb** the water that Christopher spilled.

   to soak up or take in

2. The Statue of Liberty stands on a large **pedestal**.

   a base for a statue

3. My **gullible** neighbor believed me when I said the moon is made of cheese.

   easily deceived

4. Nicholas grinned in **triumph** when he came from behind and won the race.

   a victory

5. Samantha used glue to **adhere** the sequins to her costume.

   to stick, cling, or hold tight

6. The **nomad** moved on, carrying everything he owned in a tapestry bag.

   a member of a tribe that moves from one place to another in search of food and water

7. José ran his hand over his head and said, "My hair is pretty **sparse** these days."

   not thickly grown

8. Use **disposable** party cups so we won't have any glasses to wash later.

   something made to be discarded after use

9. The jeweler agreed to **engrave** Brittany's name on her gold bracelet.

   to cut designs into a surface in an artistic way; to carve

10. Professor Garcia, a well-known **scholar** of anthropology, taught our class.

    teacher

WORD MEANINGS

Word Learning

Study the spelling, part(s) of speech, and meaning(s) of each word. Complete each sentence by writing the word on the line. Then read the sentence.

1. **absorb** *(v.)* to soak up or take in

   Kitty litter will _____ absorb _____ that oil spill on the garage floor.

2. **adhere** *(v.)* to stick, cling, or hold tight

   Double-sided tape will _____ adhere _____ posters neatly to the wall.

3. **associate** *(v.)* 1. to join in thought; 2. to join as a friend or an acquaintance; *(adj.)* connected with one or more persons or things; *(n.)* a friend, an acquaintance, or a colleague

   My cats _____ associate _____ the sound of the can opener with their dinner.

   As a new member, Jesus will begin as _____ associate _____ director of the club.

   I would like to introduce my _____ associate _____ from the office.

4. **celestial** *(adj.)* of or relating to the sky

   Do you ever look at the night sky and ponder the _____ celestial _____ bodies there?

5. **contentment** *(n.)* happiness or satisfaction

   A cup of cocoa gives me a feeling of _____ contentment _____.

6. **destiny** *(n.)* a person's fortune or fate

   It's a cowboy's _____ destiny _____ to ride the range for the rest of his life.

7. **disposable** *(adj.)* something made to be discarded after use

   Let's use _____ disposable _____ cups and plates for the picnic.

8. **engrave** *(v.)* 1. to cut designs into a surface in an artistic way; 2. to carve

   Please _____ engrave _____ "To Kaylee, with love" on this watch for my sister.

9. **frantic** *(adj.)* very excited with rage, fear, pain, or grief

   After a _____ frantic _____ search, we found the lost airline tickets.

10. **gullible** *(adj.)* 1. easily deceived; 2. unsuspecting

    The _____ gullible _____ teacher believed that Liam's pet turtle ate his homework.

11. **induce** *(v.)* 1. to influence or persuade; 2. to cause or bring about

Will counting imaginary sheep really _____induce_____ sleep?

12. **leisure** *(n.)* the time free from work in which one may rest or enjoy oneself; *(adj.)* 1. not occupied; 2. free

After this hard winter, Peter deserved three days of _____leisure_____ in Florida.

In her _____leisure_____ time, Erica likes to play chess.

13. **nomad** *(n.)* a member of a tribe that moves from one place to another in search of food and water

We met a desert _____nomad_____ who invited us to travel with his people.

14. **pedestal** *(n.)* a base for a statue or a lamp

The gallery displayed Omar's sculpture on a green marble _____pedestal_____.

15. **pigment** *(n.)* a coloring matter in the cells of plants and animals

The pink eyes of an albino rabbit are the result of a lack of _____pigment_____.

16. **radioactivity** *(n.)* the rays or tiny particles given off from atomic nuclei

Continued exposure to _____radioactivity_____ can be harmful to your health.

17. **scholar** *(n.)* 1. a student; 2. a wise person; 3. a teacher

Raymond is a dedicated _____scholar_____ who spends all his time in the library.

18. **sparse** *(adj.)* 1. thinly scattered; 2. not thickly grown

The candidate was disappointed by the _____sparse_____ crowd.

19. **triumph** *(v.)* to win success; *(n.)* a victory

The team confidently expects to _____triumph_____ over its final opponent.

Everyone celebrated the _____triumph_____ of the championship volleyball team.

20. **voluntary** *(adj.)* 1. acting on one's own choice; 2. not forced or required

Picking up litter in the park is _____voluntary_____ work.

Use Your Vocabulary

Choose the word from the Word List that best completes each sentence. Write the word on the line. You may use the plural form of nouns and the past tense of verbs if necessary.

I took my **1** time at a beach resort and was filled with **2** and a hearty seafood lunch. I imagined quitting the wandering life of a reporter, no longer living the life of a(n) **3** . I would only **4** to a schedule of sitting on the beach. Suddenly, a(n) **5** employee came running up to my chair. "Urgent telephone call," he said breathlessly.

It was Jake, my **6** at the newspaper. "Listen," he said. "There's a big story breaking. This is not a **7** assignment, and I won't have to **8** you to say yes. It's the story of the century!

"We know little; the facts are **9** . Scientific experts and university **10** are confirming that a huge meteor will hit the earth at exactly the spot where your vacation island is located.

"Grab a(n) **11** camera at the gift shop. We want pictures and a story about this **12** body hurtling down from the sky. It's your **13** that your vacation has taken you here! This story is your chance for an award. It's as if your name is already chosen and **14** on a Pulitzer Prize."

I closed my eyes to imagine how my prize would look displayed on a(n) **15** in my office.

Jake said, "They think that if the meteor hits the ocean, the water will **16** the shock. If the meteor hits land, the **17** will instantly kill every living thing. There's no hope for anyone, unless you do one thing."

"Go on," I said, getting excited. "Go on!"

"Well, cover up the **18** of your suntanned skin with yellow paint and tell everyone who will listen that you are one **19** man."

Jake laughed in **20** at his practical joke. "There's no meteor. I just called to wish you a restful vacation. See you in two weeks."

	Word List
1.	leisure
2.	contentment
3.	nomad
4.	adhere
5.	frantic
6.	associate
7.	voluntary
8.	induce
9.	sparse
10.	scholars
11.	disposable
12.	celestial
13.	destiny
14.	engraved
15.	pedestal
16.	absorb
17.	radioactivity
18.	pigment
19.	gullible
20.	triumph

SYNONYMS

Synonyms are words that have the same or nearly the same meanings.

Part 1 Choose the word from the box that is the best synonym for each group of words. Write the word on the line.

nomad	associate	adhere	sparse
triumph	scholar	pedestal	frantic

1. educated person, professor   _scholar_

2. connect; partner; joined   _associate_

3. attach, cling, bond   _adhere_

4. mad, wild, raging   _frantic_

5. wanderer, migrant, traveler   _nomad_

6. succeed, conquer; accomplishment   _triumph_

7. thin, few, scanty   _sparse_

8. stand, foundation, support   _pedestal_

Part 2 Replace the underlined word(s) with a word from the box that means the same or almost the same. Write your answer on the line.

disposable	leisure	celestial	gullible
induce	destiny	contentment	

9. Are you looking forward to a little <u>relaxation</u> time on the beach?
   leisure

10. The mother tried to <u>urge</u> her daughter to get dressed quickly.
    induce

11. Only <u>easily fooled</u> little kids could love this inept magician. _gullible_

12. Some people look to a psychic to tell them their <u>fate</u>. _destiny_

13. After the hearty meal, a feeling of <u>comfort</u> settled over the diners.
    contentment

14. Lit by twinkling lights, the dance floor transformed into a <u>heavenly</u> paradise.

_____celestial_____

15. The paper tablecloths are meant to be <u>thrown away</u>. _____disposable_____

 **ANTONYMS**

Antonyms are words that have opposite or nearly opposite meanings.

Part 1 Choose the word from the box that is the best antonym for each group of words. Write the word on the line.

frantic	adhere	contentment
voluntary	celestial	disposable

1. of the earth _____celestial_____

2. forced, controlled, compelled _____voluntary_____

3. let go, separate, loosen _____adhere_____

4. discomfort, misery, sadness _____contentment_____

5. permanent, lasting, reusable _____disposable_____

6. peaceful, calm, tranquil _____frantic_____

Part 2 Replace the underlined word(s) with a word from the box that means the opposite or almost the opposite. Write your answer on the line.

leisure	triumph	sparse
gullible	absorb	

7. Try that coin trick on my cousin. He's <u>hard to fool</u>. _____gullible_____

8. This new fabric is designed to <u>reflect</u> the rays of the sun. _____absorb_____

9. The general pointed to the <u>abundant</u> medals on his uniform.

_____sparse_____

10. The final score told the whole story of the baseball team's <u>defeat</u>.

_____triumph_____

11. Will Saturday be a day of <u>work</u> for you? _____leisure_____

WORD STUDY

Root Words Use the words in the box to complete the journal entries.

portable	portfolio	portage
transport	export	report

A Scientist's Journal

Day One: Off we go in our canoe on an important scientific mission. Our canoes are our _____ *transport* _____ into the deepest part of the rain forest. When the four of us return, we will _____ *report* _____ our findings to the medical community.

Day Two: Bad luck. We had smooth sailing until the river became a waterfall and we had to _____ *portage* _____ our canoes and equipment overland for three miles. Then our canoes capsized in rough water, and we lost our _____ *portfolio* _____ of scientific papers and a(n) _____ *portable* _____ tape recorder.

Day Three: Unbelievable success! We located the giant fungus we were looking for. Our company plans to _____ *export* _____ this fuzzy, blue fungus to foreign countries. We will be rich and famous for finding it. This fungus, we believe, will cure the common cold.

> ## Vocabulary in Action
>
> *Portage* usually refers to the act of carrying a canoe over land to avoid an obstacle on a river, such as a rapids or a waterfall. In our time of easy, convenient transportation, it is hard to imagine having to do this in order to reach our destination. But early settlers and explorers, such as Lewis and Clark, had to do this on a regular basis. Think about this the next time you cross a bridge.

CHALLENGE WORDS

Word Learning—Challenge!

Study the spelling, part of speech, and meaning(s) of each word. Complete each sentence by writing the word on the line. Then read the sentence.

1. **barren** *(adj.)* 1. not able to reproduce; 2. producing little

   We can't grow crops in this _____barren_____ soil.

2. **circumscribe** *(v.)* to construct around or mark a boundary

   To _____circumscribe_____ a square, draw a circle that touches the four corners.

3. **inconsistent** *(adj.)* lacking consistency or logic in thought or action

   Our _____inconsistent_____ weather has been cold one day and warm the next.

4. **lavish** *(adj.)* producing in abundance

   We have a _____lavish_____ supply of apples because of perfect weather.

5. **plight** *(n.)* a difficult or unfortunate situation

   A child with a broken leg is in a sad _____plight_____.

Use Your Vocabulary—Challenge!

Disaster Reporter Bad weather has turned part of your state into a disaster area. You are a newspaper reporter flying over the area in a helicopter. Your job is to describe the damage for readers. On a separate sheet of paper, write a news article about your observations. Use the Challenge Words above.

> ### Vocabulary in Action
>
> What comes to mind when you hear the word *barren*? If you said *bare*—"having nothing left over or added"— then you should be able to remember that *barren* means "not able to produce."

FUN WITH WORDS

Unscramble the letters to form words from the Word List. Then draw a line to connect each unscrambled word with its definition.

Group 1

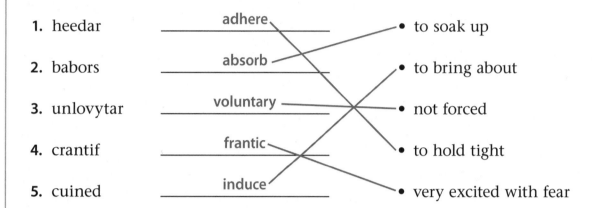

1. heedar _____ adhere • to soak up

2. babors _____ absorb • to bring about

3. unlovytar _____ voluntary • not forced

4. crantif _____ frantic • to hold tight

5. cuined _____ induce • very excited with fear

Group 2

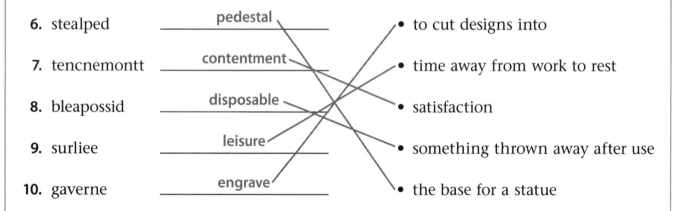

6. stealped _____ pedestal • to cut designs into

7. tencnemontt _____ contentment • time away from work to rest

8. bleapossid _____ disposable • satisfaction

9. surliee _____ leisure • something thrown away after use

10. gaverne _____ engrave • the base for a statue

Vocabulary in Action

Sometimes word spellings are exceptions to common rules of spelling. In general, the letter "i" comes before "e," except when it occurs after "c" or in words that sound like "a," such as *neighbor* and *weigh*. But the word **leisure** is an exception. Generally, you have to memorize the spellings of words like this. There is, however, a simple trick to remembering that *leisure* is spelled "ei." The first three letters of *leisure* form the word *lei*, and sometimes people wear leis when they are at leisure.

WORD LIST

Read each word using the pronunciation key.

administration (əd min i strā´ shən)
bankrupt (baŋk´ rupt)
churn (chərn)
convert (kən vərt´)
destructive (di struk´ tiv)
disrespect (dis ri spekt´)
engulf (in gulf´)
friction (frik´ shən)
gully (gul´ ē)
inept (in ept´)
liberate (lib´ ə rāt)
negotiate (ni gō´ shē āt)
obligation (ob li gā´ shən)
pioneer (pi ə nēr´)
rage (rāj)
scoundrel (skoun´ drəl)
spectrum (spek´ trəm)
splendor (splen´ dər)
trudge (truj)
warrant (wôr´ ənt)

WORD STUDY

Prefixes

These prefixes tell about number.
The prefixes *uni-* and *mono-* mean "one."
The prefix *bi-* means "two."
The prefix *tri-* means "three."

unicellular (yü nə sel´ yə lər) *(n.)* having one cell
monologue (mon´ ə lôg) *(n.)* a speech given by one person
monorail (mon´ ə rāl) *(n.)* a single rail
bicycle (bī´ sik əl) *(n.)* a vehicle with two wheels
bipolar (bī pō´ lər) *(adj.)* having two poles
triangle (trī´ aŋ gəl) *(n.)* a figure with three angles
tricolor (trī´ kul ər) *(adj.)* having three colors
tricycle (trī´ sə kəl) *(n.)* a vehicle with three wheels

Challenge Words

braggart (brag´ ərt)
corrupt (kə rupt´)
embezzle (im bez´ əl)
hardy (här´ dē)
mar (mär)

■ **TEACHER TIP: See page ix for suggestions on how to use this page.**

Level F

 # WORDS IN CONTEXT

Read each sentence below to figure out the meaning of the word in **bold**. Use reasoning skills and the remainder of the sentence to help you. Write the meaning of the word on the line.

1. The **bankrupt** woman finally admitted that she could not pay her bills.

   unable to pay debts as declared by a court of law

2. Our school district's **administration** is headed by the superintendent.

   the managing of a business, school, or office

3. Andrew's project is to **convert** his basement into a play area.

   to change from one form or use to another

4. Joseph used a mixer to **churn** the eggs, milk, and sugar.

   to stir or shake

5. The ball bearings in your skates reduce the **friction** of the moving parts.

   a scraping of one thing against another

6. The hurricane might **rage** outside, but we will be calm and safe inside.

   to act furiously

7. If waves **engulf** the rowboat, be ready to bail out the water.

   to overwhelm

8. The prism caught the sunlight and turned it to all the colors of the **spectrum**.

   a band of color formed when light is dispersed through a prism

9. I'm annoyed by people who show **disrespect** and talk throughout a movie.

   rudeness; impoliteness

10. I was barely able to **trudge** up the last hill of our long hike.

    to walk with effort

WORD MEANINGS

Word Learning

Study the spelling, part(s) of speech, and meaning(s) of each word. Complete each sentence by writing the word on the line. Then read the sentence.

1. **administration** *(n.)* 1. the managing of a business, school, or office; 2. authoritative control over the business of others

   School _____ administration _____ is not an easy task.

2. **bankrupt** *(adj.)* unable to pay debts as declared by a court of law

   Overwhelmed by its debts, the _____ bankrupt _____ business closed its doors forever.

3. **churn** *(v.)* to stir or shake

   That paint will need a good _____ churn _____ before we can start putting it on the walls.

4. **convert** *(v.)* to change from one form or use to another

   Remember to _____ convert _____ your dollars into pesos at the airport.

5. **destructive** *(adj.)* 1. devastating; 2. destroying

   The _____ destructive _____ force of a tornado can flatten buildings.

6. **disrespect** *(n.)* 1. rudeness; 2. impoliteness

   It is an act of _____ disrespect _____ to talk loudly on a cell phone in public.

7. **engulf** *(v.)* 1. to swallow up or enclose; 2. to overwhelm

   Stay in the harbor so that the waves do not _____ engulf _____ the boat.

8. **friction** *(n.)* a scraping of one thing against another

   Oil will reduce the _____ friction _____ between the parts of the engine.

9. **gully** *(n.)* a trench made by heavy rains or running water

   The pickup truck made it through the _____ gully _____ without being washed away.

10. **inept** *(adj.)* clumsy or awkward

    At first, Ashley was an _____ inept _____ ice skater, but now she is graceful.

11. **liberate** *(v.)* 1. to set free; 2. to deliver; 3. to release

    Katherine decided to _____ liberate _____ the condor back into the wild.

12. **negotiate** *(v.)* 1. to come to an agreement; 2. to talk about

The owners and players will _____negotiate_____ a new contract.

13. **obligation** *(n.)* a duty under personal feeling or law

When you receive your driver's license, you are under an _____obligation_____ to drive safely.

14. **pioneer** *(n.)* a person who settles in new territory, preparing it for others; *(v.)* to prepare or open up for others to follow

The _____pioneer_____ headed west, looking for a place to build a new home for his family.

It takes great courage to _____pioneer_____ space—the last frontier.

15. **rage** *(v.)* to speak or act furiously; *(n.)* anger; violent fury

It will not be a surprise if the protesters _____rage_____ against the city council.

Madison flew into a _____rage_____ when her sister broke her new handheld video game.

16. **scoundrel** *(n.)* a person without honor or good principles

Don't give your money to a _____scoundrel_____ who is making false promises.

17. **spectrum** *(n.)* a band of color formed when light is dispersed through a prism

A rainbow has all the colors of the _____spectrum_____.

18. **splendor** *(n.)* 1. extreme brightness; 2. magnificence

The desert is a great place to enjoy the _____splendor_____ of a sunset.

19. **trudge** *(v.)* to walk with effort

Please shovel the walk so that I do not have to _____trudge_____ through the snow.

20. **warrant** *(n.)* 1. a reason that gives a right; 2. authority; *(v.)* to justify or give a good reason for

The police had a _____warrant_____ for the escaped convict's arrest.

Do nothing that will _____warrant_____ punishment.

Use Your Vocabulary

Choose the word from the Word List that best completes each sentence. Write the word on the line. You may use the plural form of nouns and the past tense of verbs if necessary.

The newspaper reported that the zoo had run out of money and was __1__. I went straight to the office of the __2__ to talk with the zoo director. She explained that last month's __3__ storm had been very damaging to the zoo. The heavy rainfall had formed a deep, damaging __4__ in the zoo, destroying much of the landscaping. A few workers had to __5__ through ankle-deep mud in order to escape. High winds __6__ that night and caused power outages because of the __7__ between tree limbs and power lines. An uprooted tree broke a window and __8__ many rare birds.

The men hired to repair the damage turned out to be __9__ who took the zoo's money but did not complete the job. The __10__ they showed was despicable. The director explained that he was trying to __11__ with bill collectors in order to keep the zoo open. He said he has a(n) __12__ to the children of the city to keep the zoo open, but he didn't know if he could keep his commitment. The director needed help to __13__ his despair into a positive attitude. I could immediately see that the problem __14__ drastic and quick action.

I sent photographs of the wreckage to the city newspaper, hoping I could __15__ up support for an idea I had to help the zoo. I felt like such a brave __16__. My idea spread quickly. On Saturday, hundreds of volunteers from all over the city __17__ the zoo, carrying ladders, paintbrushes, saws, and hammers. We supplied paint in all the colors of the __18__. I'm a(n) __19__ painter, but I was nearly an expert by the end of the day. As the last volunteers left, I was amazed to find that the windows were mended and the mud was gone. The zoo had regained its beauty and __20__.

1. _____ bankrupt
2. _____ administration
3. _____ destructive
4. _____ gully
5. _____ trudge
6. _____ raged
7. _____ friction
8. _____ liberated
9. _____ scoundrels
10. _____ disrespect
11. _____ negotiate
12. _____ obligation
13. _____ convert
14. _____ warranted
15. _____ churn
16. _____ pioneer
17. _____ engulfed
18. _____ spectrum
19. _____ inept
20. _____ splendor

SYNONYMS

Synonyms are words that have the same or nearly the same meanings.

Part 1 Choose the word from the box that is the best synonym for each group of words. Write the word on the line.

inept	administration	friction	destructive
convert	gully	churn	engulf

1. graceless, blundering, not handy   _inept_

2. ditch, ravine   _gully_

3. rubbing of two things together   _friction_

4. flood, submerge, swamp   _engulf_

5. hurtful, harmful, causing injury   _destructive_

6. transform, alter, rework   _convert_

7. shake up, mix, beat   _churn_

8. management, supervision, guidance   _administration_

Part 2 Replace the underlined word with a word from the box that means the same or almost the same. Write your answer on the line.

rage	scoundrel	trudge	splendor
liberate	obligation	pioneer	

9. The falcon society promises to <u>free</u> all captured falcons.   _liberate_

10. You are under no <u>requirement</u> to buy more equipment from that store.   _obligation_

11. Senator John Glenn, one of the first astronauts, was a space-age <u>pathfinder</u>.   _pioneer_

12. Don't <u>show anger</u> just because that baby is being noisy.   _rage_

13. Let's find the <u>rascal</u> who broke my window.   _scoundrel_

14. I watched Stephanie <u>plod</u> up the stairs carrying a load of heavy boxes.

_____ trudge

15. Rebecca's helicopter took her over the <u>grandeur</u> of the Canadian Rocky Mountains.

_____ splendor

ANTONYMS

Antonyms are words that have opposite or nearly opposite meanings.

Part 1 Choose the word from the box that is the best antonym for each group of words. Write the word on the line.

liberate	disrespect	convert	bankrupt	inept

1. keep the same, maintain _____ convert

2. courtesy, consideration, regard _____ disrespect

3. wealthy, able to pay _____ bankrupt

4. competent, skillful, able _____ inept

5. confine, keep, restrict _____ liberate

Part 2 Replace the underlined word(s) with a word from the box that means the opposite or almost the opposite. Write your answer on the line.

churn	rage	splendor	scoundrel	trudge

6. Tyler's <u>calmness</u> really shows when he drives. _____ rage

7. As we rode our bicycles through the village, we were surprised by its <u>drabness</u>.

_____ splendor

8. I can tell how much you want to shop by the way you <u>glide</u> down the aisles of

the store. _____ trudge

9. "Show me just one <u>honest, good person</u>," said the sheriff. _____ scoundrel

10. The fishing is good where the waters <u>are calm</u>. _____ churn

WORD STUDY

Prefixes Choose the word from the box that is associated with the following words. Write the word on the line.

> unicellular   monologue   monorail   bicycle
>
> bipolar   triangle   tricolor   tricycle

1. contrasting, extremes   _____bipolar_____

2. red, white, and blue   _____tricolor_____

3. a single track   _____monorail_____

4. handlebars, seat, pedals, two wheels   _____bicycle_____

5. a wheel in front and two in back   _____tricycle_____

6. amoeba, bacterium   _____unicellular_____

7. a speech, a soliloquy   _____monologue_____

8. a musical instrument with three surfaces   _____triangle_____

Vocabulary in Action

Many know Thomas Dewey as the man whom Harry Truman defeated in the 1948 presidential election. But prior to that election, Dewey made a name for himself as a special prosecutor in New York County. One of his more prominent cases involved an **embezzlement** charge against Richard Whitney, the former president of the New York Stock Exchange. Dewey's work helped indict and convict Whitney. Later as district attorney, Dewey convicted Lucky Luciano, a well-known gangster and organized-crime leader.

CHALLENGE WORDS

Word Learning—Challenge!

Study the spelling, part(s) of speech, and meaning(s) of each word. Complete each sentence by writing the word on the line. Then read the sentence.

1. **braggart** *(n.)* one who boasts loudly

   The biggest _____braggart_____ in school is always boasting about how many trophies she has.

2. **corrupt** *(v.)* to change from good to bad in values or actions; *(adj.)* characterized by morally wrong behavior

   Don't _____corrupt_____ honest people by tempting them to break laws.

   The _____corrupt_____ taxi driver charged his passengers twice the normal rate.

3. **embezzle** *(v.)* to use others' money or property for one's own personal gain

   The bank teller had a plan to _____embezzle_____ money by hiding it in her purse.

4. **hardy** *(adj.)* 1. capable of withstanding harsh conditions; 2. brave

   This _____hardy_____ little car pulled a trailer through snow and ice.

5. **mar** *(v.)* to injure, harm, or destroy

   A sharp object may _____mar_____ the beautiful wooden tabletop.

Use Your Vocabulary—Challenge!

Thief Caught You are a police officer. You have arrested a stranger for stealing money from a charity. On a separate sheet of paper, write a police report on this arrest. Use the Challenge Words above. Be sure to tell what the crime was and how it was committed.

> ### Vocabulary in Action
>
> *Monologue* was originally a French word that dated back to the mid-1500s. It was produced by combining *mon* ("one, single, alone") and *logue* ("discourse, talk").

FUN WITH WORDS

There are 10 words from the Word List hidden in this puzzle. The words may run across, up, down, forward, backward, or diagonally. Find each word and circle it. Then write five sentences using at least one word in each sentence.

```
E T P B A N K E P T T I O N T R U M W
T D A A A D M I N I S T R A T I O N U
A E N N C H J L W A N E B S A G C O T
R R E K O F X M A I N E P T F U H I S
E O E R L U V M R Z Y X G L L L C T L
B A R U Q T U N R E L E L O K L O C K
I N G P P R P I A E R E L L T Y N I J
L R U T T W A R N S E L E R D I D R C
R X L C O N V R T R U D G E U O A F B
I W E N G L L G E T C E P S E D S T A
S P I O G A R N O I T A G I L B O M E
S S U A E I O Y F R C T N L I P B I L
```

1. Answers will vary.

_____

_____

2. _____

_____

3 _____

_____

4. _____

_____

5. _____

_____

Review 4–6

Word Meanings Fill in the bubble of the word that is best defined by each phrase.

1. feel scorn for
   a. displace   **b. despise**   c. engrave   d. liberate

2. shining brightly
   a. radiant   b. acute   c. scant   d. celestial

3. a lack of politeness
   a. contentment   b. destiny   **c. disrespect**   d. obligation

4. easily tricked
   a. physical   b. disposable   **c. gullible**   d. bankrupt

5. not thick or crowded
   a. sparse   b. voluntary   c. destructive   d. inept

6. an early settler
   a. scholar   b. nobility   c. pedestal   **d. pioneer**

7. not with others
   a. leisure   **b. solitary**   c. physical   d. celestial

8. impossible to understand
   a. frantic   b. bankrupt   c. voluntary   **d. incomprehensible**

9. to take in
   a. churn   b. trifle   c. induce   **d. absorb**

10. a big victory
    a. crystal   **b. triumph**   c. pedestal   d. friction

11. to let go
    a. convert   b. trudge   **c. liberate**   d. flex

12. to talk over a problem
    a. displace   b. engulf   **c. negotiate**   d. associate

13. a feeling of great anger
    a. splendor   b. obligation   **c. rage**   d. trifle

14. grateful or thankful
    a. appreciative   b. destructive   c. sparse   d. incomprehensible

15. to remain attached
    a. rage   b. despise   c. warrant   **d. adhere**

16. wild with worry
    a. radiant   **b. frantic**   c. solitary   d. inept

17. the space something takes up
    a. gully   **b. volume**   c. leisure   d. enforcement

18. bungling or clumsy
    (a.) destructive   (b.) frantic   (c.) inept   (d.) gullible

19. shininess
    (a.) volume   (b.) destiny   (c.) radioactivity   (d.) sheen

20. the act of directing a business or an office
    (a.) administration   (b.) spectrum   (c.) obligation   (d.) friction

Sentence Completion Choose the word from the box that best completes each of the following sentences. Write the word in the blank.

associate	converts	disposable	cavity	induce
consider	voluntary	engraved	legislate	scant

1. The deep _____cavity_____ in the tree trunk was caused by a lightning strike.

2. Our team received the championship trophy with "First Place" _____engraved_____ on it.

3. Don't _____associate_____ with people who spread gossip about others.

4. A mill _____converts_____ wheat grain into flour.

5. You should _____consider_____ what the world would be like if we all treated one another the way we want to be treated.

6. Some people say we live in a "throwaway" world because we use so many _____disposable_____ products.

7. Such a(n) _____scant_____ amount of food will not feed all these people.

8. We elect people to Congress to _____legislate_____ for our country.

9. Participating in the project is _____voluntary_____; we aren't trying to force people to take part.

10. Can't we _____induce_____ you to join the team?

Fill in the Blanks Fill in the bubble of the pair of words that best completes each sentence.

1. The sheriff issued a(n) _____ for the _____ arrest.
    (a.) enforcement, pioneer's   (c.) pedestal, scholar's
    (b.) warrant, scoundrel's   (d.) obligation, associate's

2. The _____ of the view gave me a feeling of _____.

   a. administration, rage   **c.** splendor, contentment

   b. nobility, radioactivity   **d.** triumph, leisure

3. Mud and vapor shot out of the volcano's glowing _____ just before the mountain was _____ in boiling lava.

   a. cavity, engulfed   **c.** gully, liberated

   b. pedestal, adhered   **d.** crystal, absorbed

4. I enjoy the _____ life of a writer, but I also enjoy spending time with my _____.

   a. destructive, nomads   **c.** inept, administration

   b. incomprehensible, scoundrels   **d.** solitary, associates

5. Taylor thinks a career in law _____ is her _____.

   a. contentment, triumph   **c.** enforcement, destiny

   b. disrespect, obligation   **d.** administration, leisure

6. The _____ will attempt to _____ a new contract.

   a. pioneer, adhere   **c.** nomad, legislate

   b. administration, negotiate   **d.** nobility, despise

7. We saw all the colors of the _____ in the _____ light show of a meteor shower.

   a. friction, gullible   **c.** pigment, voluntary

   b. spectrum, celestial   **d.** splendor, bankrupt

8. Nothing can _____ me to break the promise I made to my _____.

   a. induce, associate   **c.** liberate, crystal

   b. displace, warrant   **d.** churn, pioneers

9. Using too many _____ products is _____ to our environment.

   a. radiant, acute   **c.** sparse, physical

   b. voluntary, appreciative   **d.** disposable, destructive

10. No one is allowed to show _____ to a member of the _____.

   a. obligation, pioneers   **c.** disrespect, nobility

   b. triumph, gully   **d.** rage, cavity

Classifying Words
Sort the words in the box by writing each word to complete a phrase in the correct category.

administration	appreciative	associates	contentment	crystal
despise	disrespect	enforcement	gulf	gully
liberate	negotiate	nomad	obligations	physical
pioneers	rage	scholar	scoundrel's	sparse

Words You Might Use to Talk About People

1. give credit to your coworkers and _____ associates _____
2. enjoy the traveling life of a(n) _____ nomad _____
3. show the brilliant education of a(n) _____ scholar _____
4. admire the bravery of our country's first _____ pioneers _____
5. put an end to the _____ scoundrel's _____ bad deeds

Words You Might Use to Talk About Feelings

6. smile because you're _____ appreciative _____ of your birthday gifts
7. _____ despise _____ people who do cruel things
8. give a sigh of _____ contentment _____ in front of the cozy fire
9. try to control your feelings of _____ rage _____
10. showed _____ disrespect _____ by the tone of her voice

Words You Might Use to Talk About Geography

11. see the terrain on a(n) _____ physical _____ map
12. go snorkeling in the _____ gulf _____
13. see forests become _____ sparse _____ as you get near the tundra
14. the sun shining down on a(n) _____ crystal _____ clear lake
15. a(n) _____ gully _____ cut into the rock by running water

Words You Might Use to Talk About Government

16. working to _____ liberate _____ oppressed people everywhere
17. a new _____ administration _____ in power after the election
18. the president's _____ obligations _____ to do the work of the people
19. ambassadors trying to _____ negotiate _____ peace treaties
20. _____ enforcement _____ of laws to keep citizens safe

CHAPTER 7

WORD LIST

Read each word using the pronunciation key.

adventurous (ad ven´ chər əs)
beacon (bē´ kən)
civilize (siv´ i līz)
correspond (kôr i spond´)
detach (di tach´)
dissolve (di zolv´)
enlist (en list´)
gaseous (gas´ ē əs)
harbor (här´ bər)
inevitable (in ev´ i tə bəl)
literal (lit´ ər əl)
nonabrasive (non´ ə brā siv)
obscure (əb skyŏŏr´)
pedestrian (pə des´ trē ən)
pore (pôr)
react (rē akt´)
serene (sə rēn´)
sprawl (sprôl)
uphold (up hōld´)
weave (wēv)

WORD STUDY

Suffixes

The suffix *-ic* means "having the characteristic of" or "relating to."

angelic (an jel´ ik) *(adj.)* like an angel
artistic (är tis´ tik) *(adj.)* of art or artists
athletic (ath let´ ik) *(adj.)* like an athlete
dramatic (drə mat´ ik) *(adj.)* having to do with plays
historic (hi stôr´ ik) *(adj.)* important in history
photographic (fō tə graf´ ik) *(adj.)* relating to photography

Challenge Words

cater (kā´ tər)
dialogue (dī´ ə lôg)
expendable (ik spen´ də bəl)
magnitude (mag´ ni tŏŏd)
regime (rə zhēm´)

■ **TEACHER TIP:** See page ix for suggestions on how to use this page.

WORDS IN CONTEXT

Read each sentence below to figure out the meaning of the word in **bold**. Use reasoning skills and the remainder of the sentence to help you. Write the meaning of the word on the line.

1. Faced with the **inevitable** sinking of their ship, the sailors swam for shore.

   something that is sure or certain

2. Before you fix a broken caboose, **detach** it from the rest of the train.

   to remove or unfasten

3. High waves prevented the ships from leaving the safe **harbor**.

   a sheltered place for ships

4. When six-foot Daniel **sprawled** on the couch, no one else could sit down.

   to spread out in an irregular or awkward manner

5. This **nonabrasive** cleanser gently cleans the kitchen counter without scratching.

   not causing irritation

6. Every week since she moved to Dubai, I **correspond** with Jessica by mail.

   to exchange letters with another

7. Amber will **uphold** family tradition by becoming a dentist like her mother.

   to support

8. At night, tall buildings are illuminated with a red **beacon** so low-flying aircraft can see them.

   a light used as a signal to warn or guide

9. Aaron had no time to **react** as the tennis ball flew past him.

   to respond to something or someone

10. The town's **serene** atmosphere changed when the circus arrived.

    peaceful

WORD MEANINGS

Word Learning

Study the spelling, part(s) of speech, and meaning(s) of each word. Complete each sentence by writing the word on the line. Then read the sentence.

1. **adventurous** *(adj.)* 1. fond of risk; 2. full of hazard or danger

    My _____adventurous_____ sister returned from the woods claiming she'd found a cave.

2. **beacon** *(n.)* a light used as a signal to warn or guide

    The lighthouse _____beacon_____ guided the ship toward the harbor.

3. **civilize** *(v.)* to advance from a primitive way of life

    Kristina is trying to _____civilize_____ Abraham by telling him not to eat with his fingers.

4. **correspond** *(v.)* 1. to agree; 2. to exchange letters with another

    I _____correspond_____ with a girl in Japan, and I eagerly await her letters.

5. **detach** *(v.)* 1. to remove or unfasten; 2. to separate

    Would you _____detach_____ the house key from your key chain and give it to me?

6. **dissolve** *(v.)* 1. to become liquid; 2. to end

    The soap powder will _____dissolve_____ in warm water.

7. **enlist** *(v.)* 1. to get help; 2. to secure support and aid; 3. to voluntarily go into the armed forces or another group

    If math is puzzling you, then please _____enlist_____ a tutor to help you study.

8. **gaseous** *(adj.)* in a form that has neither a definite shape nor volume

    After the volcano erupted, all that remained was a _____gaseous_____ cloud of vapor.

9. **harbor** *(n.)* a sheltered place for ships; *(v.)* to provide shelter to

    Fishing is allowed only off the pier in the _____harbor_____.

    Douglas offered to _____harbor_____ the orphaned fox pups.

10. **inevitable** *(adj.)* 1. something that is sure or certain; 2. unavoidable

    With our score so high, I think that victory is _____inevitable_____.

11. literal *(adj.)* 1. word for word; 2. exact; 3. precise

A _____literal_____ translation is not as beautiful as reading the poem in French.

12. nonabrasive *(adj.)* not causing irritation

Use a _____nonabrasive_____ cleanser on your glasses or you will regret it.

13. obscure *(adj.)* 1. unknown; 2. unclear; *(v.)* 1. to hide from view; 2. to dim or darken

Caroline gives such _____obscure_____ directions that I can never find her house.

Overgrown shrubbery and vines _____obscure_____ the secret door.

14. pedestrian *(n.)* 1. one who walks; 2. a person who travels by foot

The _____pedestrian_____ waited for traffic to pass before crossing the street.

15. pore *(n.)* a very tiny opening; *(v.)* to gaze at or examine long and steadily

Angel could feel the healing cream seep into each _____pore_____ of his skin.

Just before a big test, Gabriella and Colton _____pore_____ over their notes.

16. react *(v.)* to respond to something or someone

When you hear the alarm, I want each of you to _____react_____ quickly.

17. serene *(adj.)* 1. peaceful; 2. calm; 3. quiet

A summer sunrise puts Hope in a _____serene_____ mood.

18. sprawl *(v.)* to spread out in an irregular or awkward manner

Because there are no chairs left, you can _____sprawl_____ on the floor.

19. uphold *(v.)* 1. to support; 2. to not let down

The police will take extra care this weekend to _____uphold_____ the law.

20. weave *(v.)* 1. to go by twisting and turning; 2. to interlace threads to make a cloth

A New Year's dragon will _____weave_____ through the streets of Chinatown.

Use Your Vocabulary

Choose the word from the Word List that best completes each sentence. Write the word on the line. You may use the plural form of nouns and the past tense of verbs if necessary.

Curtis and Israel, two __1__ boys who loved excitement, decided to spend Saturday exploring the ships and shoreline of the city __2__ . They __3__ the aid of their older sister, Sandra. "Of course I'll take you," Sandra said. "Someone has to __4__ you two rascals and be sure you behave."

So off they went on foot, three __5__ who were quite certain that they would find the __6__ adventure. At the pier, Sandra __7__ the pack from her waist and pulled out a guidebook. While she __8__ over the book, the boys stood on the pier watching jet skis __9__ around the buoys. "Yuck," they said as a(n) __10__ cloud erupted from the smokestack of an old steamship. They could also see people at the old lighthouse that once served as a(n) __11__ to incoming ships. The boys looked at each other and at the same time their thoughts __12__ : The lighthouse was open! They expected Sandra to balk and __13__ with a firm "No way," but Sandra, determined to __14__ her role as older sister, led the way.

Some of the boys' energy __15__ as they trudged up and up the circular stairway. As they huffed and puffed, they vaguely remembered some __16__ purpose they had for climbing to the top, but it no longer seemed important. When they finally reached the top, the view of the buildings and streets __17__ below them to the west and the gentle roll of the calm ocean to the east cast a(n) __18__ feeling over all of them.

They learned that the shiny brass lantern housing the great light was polished each day with a(n) __19__ cleanser to remove corrosive salt spray. And they learned that the __20__ translation of the Latin words on the side of the lantern was "I light the way."

1. _____ adventurous _____
2. _____ harbor _____
3. _____ enlisted _____
4. _____ civilize _____
5. _____ pedestrians _____
6. _____ inevitable _____
7. _____ detached _____
8. _____ pored _____
9. _____ weave _____
10. _____ gaseous _____
11. _____ beacon _____
12. _____ corresponded _____
13. _____ react _____
14. _____ uphold _____
15. _____ dissolved _____
16. _____ obscure _____
17. _____ sprawled _____
18. _____ serene _____
19. _____ nonabrasive _____
20. _____ literal _____

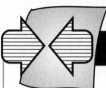

SYNONYMS

Synonyms are words that have the same or nearly the same meanings.

Part 1 Choose the word from the box that is the best synonym for each group of words. Write the word on the line.

enlist	pore	sprawl	uphold
inevitable	correspond	harbor	obscure

1. gain assistance   _____enlist_____

2. lounge, slouch   _____sprawl_____

3. vague, uncertain; conceal   _____obscure_____

4. inescapable, sure to happen   _____inevitable_____

5. agree, communicate   _____correspond_____

6. port, wharf; shield, protect   _____harbor_____

7. maintain, sustain, defend   _____uphold_____

8. tiny hole; inspect, survey   _____pore_____

Part 2 Replace the underlined word with a word from the box that means the same or almost the same. Write your answer on the line.

adventurous	beacon	detach	dissolve
literal	nonabrasive	serene	

9. The shoulder straps <u>disconnect</u> on some backpacks. _____detach_____

10. The <u>undisturbed</u> beauty of the Texas hills can be seen best from horseback.
_____serene_____

11. Who changes the light bulb in the <u>signal</u> on top of the Sears Tower?
_____beacon_____

12. My favorite candy claims to <u>melt</u> in my mouth, not in my hand.
_____dissolve_____

13. The newspaper claimed to have a <u>real</u> account by an eyewitness.

_____literal_____

14. Johnathan undertook a <u>bold</u> journey in a hot-air balloon. _____adventurous_____

15. Sergio has a <u>soothing</u> voice. _____nonabrasive_____

ANTONYMS

Antonyms are words that have opposite or nearly opposite meanings.

Part 1 Choose the word from the box that is the best antonym for each group of words. Write the word on the line.

weave	obscure	detach	serene	enlist

1. troubled, rough, excited _____serene_____

2. attach, bind, connect _____detach_____

3. make a beeline, go straight as an arrow _____weave_____

4. obvious, well known; expose, show _____obscure_____

5. reject, refuse, not ask for _____enlist_____

Part 2 Replace the underlined word with a word from the box that means the opposite or almost the opposite. Write your answer on the line.

correspond	adventurous	nonabrasive	literal	inevitable

6. It's a <u>routine</u> climb to the top of this mountain.

_____adventurous_____

7. The debaters changed their opinions so that they would <u>disagree</u>.

_____correspond_____

8. Alejandra revealed the <u>figurative</u> meaning of her story. _____literal_____

9. With your grades, it is <u>uncertain</u> that you will be on the honor roll.

_____inevitable_____

10. Kylee's <u>irritating</u> personality is unforgettable. _____nonabrasive_____

WORD STUDY

Suffixes Choose the word from the box that best completes each phrase. Write your answer on the line.

historic	athletic	photographic
artistic	angelic	dramatic

1. A child who is very kind and sweet-natured: a(n) _____angelic_____ child

2. An ability to play and excel at sports: a(n) _____athletic_____ ability

3. A community where many writers and painters live: a(n) _____artistic_____ community

4. A play that has a serious theme: a(n) _____dramatic_____ play

5. A place that helps us understand the past: a(n) _____historic_____ place

6. A process that develops pictures made by a camera: a(n) _____photographic_____ process

Vocabulary in Action

Drama comes from the Greek word that means "action." Dramas may be performed in various media, including theater, radio, film, and television. As indicated on page 75, ***dramatic*** usually means "having to do with plays." For this reason, a person may be called *dramatic* if he or she is overly emotional. Recently, the terms *drama queen* and *drama king* have become popular in referring to someone who is very expressive.

CHALLENGE WORDS

Word Learning—Challenge!

Study the spelling, part of speech, and meaning(s) of each word. Complete each sentence by writing the word on the line. Then read the sentence.

1. **cater** *(v.)* to supply or provide what is required

   We have all the food we need to _____cater_____ your party for you.

2. **dialogue** *(n.)* 1. an exchange of words between persons; 2. a conversation

   The referee and the coach had an angry _____dialogue_____ about the final score.

3. **expendable** *(adj.)* normally used and easily replaced

   The teacher considers pencils and paper to be _____expendable_____ supplies.

4. **magnitude** *(n.)* the importance or quality of something

   This prize-winning entry is a poem of the highest _____magnitude_____.

5. **regime** *(n.)* 1. regular pattern or process of action; 2. a form of government

   The president's new _____regime_____ begins when he takes the oath of office.

Use Your Vocabulary—Challenge!

A Strange Land Imagine that you are making a movie about a strange, faraway place. On a separate sheet of paper, write a journal entry about your adventures using the Challenge Words above. Be sure to describe the place, the people, and their strange customs.

Notable Quotes

"The consequences of things are not always proportionate to the apparent **magnitude** of those events that have produced them. Thus the American Revolution, from which little was expected, produced much; but the French Revolution, from which much was expected, produced little."

—Charles Caleb Cotton (1780–1832), British sportsman, writer

FUN WITH WORDS

The nation of Varon has just discovered a group of rare land whales living on a nearby island. The whales would like to move to the mainland, but they're scared of the ocean and refuse to swim over. Varon's leaders have decided to build a bridge from the mainland to the whales' island.

You have been called in to build the bridge with the vocabulary words from this chapter. Read the definitions below, and place the correct vocabulary words in the blank bridge spaces provided. When you have supplied all the definitions, the land whales will be able to cross safely.

Across

4. to change to a liquid
5. to respond
8. doesn't irritate
10. precise

Down

1. having no defined size or shape
2. to have the same opinion
3. a signal light
6. to educate and advance
7. to give shelter
9. to spread out

WORD LIST

Read each word using the pronunciation key.

advisable (ad vī′ zə bəl)
besiege (bi sēj′)
clarity (klâr′ i tē)
corridor (kôr′ i dər)
detect (di tekt′)
distort (di stôrt′)
enrage (en rāj′)
gasp (gasp)
impede (im pēd′)
initiative (i nish′ ə tiv)
mangle (maŋ′ gəl)
observation (ob zər vā′ shən)
persuasion (pər swā′ zhən)
posterity (pä stâr′ ə tē)
rebel (*n., adj.* reb′ əl)(*v.,* ri bel′)
shaft (shaft)
stamina (stam′ ə nə)
timid (ti′ mid)
urban (ər′ bən)
whisk (hwisk)

WORD STUDY

Prefixes

The prefix *post-* means "after" or "later."

postdate (pōst dāt′) *(v.)* to give a later date
postgraduate (pōst gra′ jə wət) *(adj.)* continuing school after high school or college
postpone (pōst pōn′) *(v.)* to put off until later
postscript (pōst′ skript) *(n.)* a message written after the writer's name has been signed to a piece of correspondence
posttest (pōst′ test) *(n.)* a test given after something is taught
postwar (pōst′ wôr′) *(adj.)* after a war

Challenge Words

clamor (klam′ ər)
denote (di nōt′)
dynasty (dī′ nə stē)
paradox (pâr′ ə doks)
utmost (ut′ mōst)

■ **TEACHER TIP:** See page ix for suggestions on how to use this page.

Level F

WORDS IN CONTEXT

Read each sentence below to figure out the meaning of the word in **bold**. Use reasoning skills and the remainder of the sentence to help you. Write the meaning of the word on the line.

1. Elizabeth laughs when the warped funhouse mirrors **distort** her reflection.

   to change shape by pushing, pulling, or twisting

2. Brandon's efforts to **impede** the growth of weeds in his yard were unsuccessful.

   to interfere with

3. Our grandmother could **detect** a visitor even before the doorbell rang.

   to discover

4. It takes **initiative** for Eric to wake up at 4:30 a.m. to practice gymnastics.

   an active or energetic part in beginning any undertaking

5. My brothers **enrage** me when they tease me about my boyfriend.

   to fill with anger

6. We tried to **whisk** away all signs of the food fight before my parents returned.

   to move rapidly

7. The runner's incredible **stamina** allowed her to complete the three-day race.

   endurance

8. The moving van rolled over Jason's bike and **mangled** it.

   to cut or tear with great force

9. Caleb stayed underwater too long and had to **gasp** for air.

   to try to get one's breath

10. Random guessing is not an **advisable** course of action for a final exam.

    wise

WORD MEANINGS

Word Learning

Study the spelling, part(s) of speech, and meaning(s) of each word. Complete each sentence by writing the word on the line. Then read the sentence.

1. **advisable** *(adj.)* 1. sensible; 2. wise; 3. proper

   Savannah hopes to reach an _____advisable_____ decision on which car to buy.

2. **besiege** *(v.)* to crowd around someone or something in an effort to capture

   The armies from the west had come to _____besiege_____ the fortress.

3. **clarity** *(n.)* the condition of being clear and understandable

   Kelsey spoke with great _____clarity_____, and for the first time I understood fractions.

4. **corridor** *(n.)* a long passage or hallway that leads into open rooms

   Go up the stairs, walk down the _____corridor_____, and open the back door.

5. **detect** *(v.)* 1. to discover; 2. to learn

   Turn down the radio; I think I _____detect_____ a strange noise outside.

6. **distort** *(v.)* 1. to change shape by pushing, pulling, or twisting; 2. to twist something from its true meaning

   This mask is great because I can _____distort_____ the shape of the nose.

7. **enrage** *(v.)* 1. to fill with anger; 2. to make mad

   Do not _____enrage_____ the caged lion by blowing that whistle.

8. **gasp** *(v.)* to try to get one's breath

   I had to _____gasp_____ for air after running the marathon.

9. **impede** *(v.)* 1. to interfere with; 2. to obstruct

   Today's heavy rainfall will _____impede_____ our camping trip.

10. **initiative** *(n.)* an active or energetic part in beginning any undertaking

    The quarterback took the _____initiative_____ when his team was behind.

11. **mangle** *(v.)* to cut or tear with great force

    Set the washer on delicate or it might _____mangle_____ your silk blouse.

12. **observation** *(n.)* 1. the act of watching and noting; 2. a remark or comment

    Marissa's _____observation_____ that good weather was coming was true.

87

13. persuasion *(n.)* the process of convincing someone to do or believe something

To get a raise in her allowance, Breanna needs to use gentle _____persuasion_____.

14. posterity *(n.)* 1. future generations; 2. all of one's offspring

For the sake of _____posterity_____, do not cut down the oak trees.

15. rebel *(n.)* a person who defies or fights against someone of authority instead of obeying; *(adj.)* resisting law or authority; *(v.)* 1. to defy or fight against the law of authority; 2. to feel a great dislike or opposition of someone or something

After Bryan dyed his hair green, his friends called him a _____rebel_____.

Many soldiers were killed in the _____rebel_____ uprising.

Do you expect Alicia to _____rebel_____ against the new rule?

16. shaft *(n.)* a long, narrow passage that is similar to a well

The miners stood at the top of the _____shaft_____ and discussed their next move.

17. stamina *(n.)* endurance or strength

Long-distance swimmers need to build up a great deal of _____stamina_____.

18. timid *(adj.)* lacking courage

My _____timid_____ uncle is frightened by loud noises.

19. urban *(adj.)* of or relating to cities or towns

Kylie chose to live in an _____urban_____ community instead of on a farm.

20. whisk *(n.)* 1. a rapid sweep; 2. a light, rapid movement; *(v.)* to move rapidly

With a _____whisk_____ of her jeweled hand, the princess dismissed her servants.

Let's _____whisk_____ the broom across the floor and clean this place quickly.

Vocabulary in Action

Harriet Tubman is best known for helping slaves flee along the Underground Railroad. But Tubman also helped the Union army win the Civil War. Because she knew the land from working along the Underground Railroad, Tubman was especially helpful to the Union as a spy. She recruited a group of former slaves to hunt for **rebel** camps and report on the movement of Confederate troops.

Use Your Vocabulary

Choose the word from the Word List that best completes each sentence. Write the word on the line. You may use the plural form of nouns and the past tense of verbs if necessary.

Doors __1__ open and closed with a swoosh as Shane angrily walked down the long __2__ of the starship. He had just learned that a report to the command center had __3__ facts about his leadership. The report said the following:

- that he had used poor judgment in befriending a remote alien race
- that __4__ action would have been to __5__ the colony and destroy its populated __6__ areas
- that he had ignored all logic and the only __7__ he had listened to was the voice of his cowardice

The report __8__ Shane, but that did not prevent him from thinking with __9__ .

Just two years ago, Shane was congratulated for taking the __10__ to visit the government of a formerly hostile race. His careful __11__ of the situation later helped make them an ally.

Now someone was trying to __12__ his crew's mission and destroy and __13__ his good reputation with lies. He had heard rumors that his second lieutenant, Jada, wanted to be starship captain. Maybe she wanted to be captain at all costs.

Shane arrived at Jada's cabin. It seemed empty, but his scan tool __14__ a faint noise from the open vent of a pressurizing shaft. "Jada, I know you're here, and I know I have the __15__ to survive any attack you can make on me," Shane said.

He heard someone __16__ for breath. Then a small, __17__ voice from the __18__ said, "How did you know it was me?"

"The postscript on the bottom of the report was in your handwriting," Shane said. "Jada, you are dismissed from this crew. There is no room on this starship for a(n) __19__ who causes trouble only for her own benefit. The work we do is for all __20__ ."

1. _____ whisked _____
2. _____ corridors _____
3. _____ distorted _____
4. _____ advisable _____
5. _____ besiege _____
6. _____ urban _____
7. _____ persuasion _____
8. _____ enraged _____
9. _____ clarity _____
10. _____ initiative _____
11. _____ observation _____
12. _____ impede _____
13. _____ mangle _____
14. _____ detected _____
15. _____ stamina _____
16. _____ gasp _____
17. _____ timid _____
18. _____ shaft _____
19. _____ rebel _____
20. _____ posterity _____

SYNONYMS

Synonyms are words that have the same or nearly the same meanings.

Part 1 Choose the word from the box that is the beset synonym for each group of words. Write the word on the line.

> impede   rebel   enrage   besiege   clarity   detect   initiative

1. revolutionary; rise up; defiant _____rebel_____

2. aggravate, inflame, madden _____enrage_____

3. block, stop, deter _____impede_____

4. storm, try to capture _____besiege_____

5. first step, introductory act _____initiative_____

6. observe, notice, perceive _____detect_____

7. plainness, simplicity _____clarity_____

Part 2 Replace the underlined word with a word from the box that means the same or almost the same. Write your answer on the line.

> stamina   mangle   advisable   gasp
> whisk   observation distort   corridor

8. After years of <u>viewing</u>, the astronomer discovered a new star.
_____observation_____

9. The firefighter had to <u>gulp</u> for air when he came out of the smoke-filled building.
_____gasp_____

10. The video game instructions say it is <u>recommended</u> to start playing at the Easy setting. _____advisable_____

11. A lawn mower that is working poorly will <u>damage</u> the grass instead of cut it.
_____mangle_____

12. Alexis wished he had the <u>energy</u> to swim across the lake. _____stamina_____

13. Hayley wanted to <u>speed</u> herself away to a sunny beach. _____whisk_____

14. Every door in the hotel's long <u>hall</u> looked alike. _____corridor_____

15. The heat from the radiator will <u>deform</u> any nearby plastic toys.
_____distort_____

 **ANTONYMS**

Antonyms are words that have opposite or nearly opposite meanings.

Part 1 Choose the word from the box that is the best antonym for each group of words. Write the word on the line.

advisable	stamina	distort	impede	whisk

1. weakness, lack of power _____stamina_____

2. crawl, drag; slow motion _____whisk_____

3. keep in proper form _____distort_____

4. not recommended, improper _____advisable_____

5. promote, open the way for _____impede_____

Part 2 Replace the underlined word with a word from the box that means the opposite or almost the opposite. Write your answer on the line.

clarity	enrage	rebel	urban	posterity

6. Roberto wondered why music always seemed to <u>calm</u> the horses.
_____enrage_____

7. <u>Rural</u> houses come in all different shapes and sizes. _____urban_____

8. When King George's laws were read aloud, some colonists decided to <u>submit</u>.
_____rebel_____

9. The new schedule resulted in greater <u>confusion</u> in the operation of the school.
_____clarity_____

10. Gage claims that he takes <u>his ancestors</u> into consideration with every decision he makes. _____posterity_____

WORD STUDY

Prefixes Choose the word from the box that best completes each pair of sentences. Write the word in the blank.

postgraduate	postscript	postwar
posttest	postpone	postdate

1. There were lots of jobs and money after World War II. It was _____postwar_____ prosperity.

2. After high school, Holly decided to attend college. She wanted to do _____postgraduate_____ work in the field of medicine.

3. Emmanuel will write a check today, but put tomorrow's date on it. He will _____postdate_____ the check.

4. Kendall wrote a note at the end of her letter. The _____postscript_____ said, "P.S. I love you."

5. We can't go to the theater tonight because of the weather. We will need to _____postpone_____ our plans.

6. Larry is able to skip the sixth grade math book. He performed so well on the fifth grade _____posttest_____ that he has advanced to the seventh grade math book.

Notable Quotes

"When we are planning for **posterity**, we ought to remember that virtue is not hereditary."

—Thomas Paine (1737–1809), British intellectual, revolutionary

CHALLENGE WORDS

Word Learning—Challenge!

Study the spelling, part(s) of speech, and meaning(s) of each word. Complete each sentence by writing the word on the line. Then read the sentence.

1. **clamor** *(n.)* loud noise; *(v.)* to make a loud noise

   The lawn mower made such a _____ clamor _____ that it woke me up.

   My baby brothers _____ clamor _____ for food if they're not fed on time.

2. **denote** *(v.)* 1. to stand for or signify; 2. to designate

   We _____ denote _____ poison with a drawing of a skull and crossbones.

3. **dynasty** *(n.)* a series of rulers from the same family or group

   A _____ dynasty _____ of kings has ruled the country for a thousand years.

4. **paradox** *(n.)* something or someone that has contradictory qualities

   A friendly enemy is a real _____ paradox _____.

5. **utmost** *(adj.)* the highest attainable point

   I will need your _____ utmost _____ cooperation to finish this job on time.

Use Your Vocabulary—Challenge!

Time Traveler Imagine that you have traveled back in time. The ruler of an ancient civilization asked you to solve a serious problem affecting a great number of people. Using the Challenge Words above, write a letter to a friend telling what happened. Be sure to describe the problem and how you helped to solve it.

> ### Vocabulary in Action
>
> The word **paradox** is from the Latin *paradoxum*, which is from the Greek *paradoxon*. In the original Greek, dating to 1540, the word meant "contrary to expectation."

FUN WITH WORDS

Hidden among the letters below are 11 of your vocabulary words from this chapter. They are written backward, forward, up, down, and diagonally. Your task is to find all the words and circle them. Hint: To know which words to look for, fill in the correct words next to the clues.

Clues

1. resisting law or authority _____ rebel

2. to tear with great force _____ mangle

3. to find out _____ detect

4. a long, thin tunnel _____ shaft

5. not brave _____ timid

6. to try to get one's breath _____ gasp

7. of or relating to cities _____ urban

8. a long hallway _____ corridor

9. to obstruct _____ impede

10. the state of being clear _____ clarity

11. to make mad _____ enrage

```
T V E J U N R S Z W O I E E R S
M F L H J Y F Z E U Y D M N E C
N O G I E F E D E T X S E B B E
T O N H W J G L I G E T D Y E U
I D A U B R S R E I A B U U L A
M B M W S K A C D W I R H K S B
I U E Q U L V B O K B E N T U T
D M F H C H U Y D A S N M E G C
Y R T U K O J I N C T X O G C E
M S J F I E R F A S B Y V O T T
W Y U U A G L R S N I M P E D E
E K K W O H O T I O D G R S E D
G U I D N S S R E D V R E C E O
C P S A G N Y U V L O G R O P T
I B G E M U I F E A V R G E A T
T S J F E A B H I U N R O S Y V
```

WORD LIST

Read each word using the pronunciation key.

aerial (âr´ ē əl)
blight (blīt)
classification (klas ə fə kā´ shən)
council (koun´ səl)
debate (di bāt´)
deter (di tər´)
division (di vizh´ ən)
entangle (en taŋ´ gəl)
generate (jen´ ə rāt)
horde (hôrd)
inquire (in kwīr´)
manipulate (mə nip´ yə lāt)
obstacle (ob´ stə kəl)
perspective (pər spek´ tiv)
precaution (pri kô´ shən)
recuperate (ri ko͞o´ pə rāt)
shed (shed)
stir (stər)
valiant (val´ yənt)
wholesome (hōl´ səm)

WORD STUDY

Analogies

Analogies show relationships between pairs of words. Study the relationships between the pairs of words in the analogies below.

give is to **receive** as **save** is to **spend**

chick is to **hen** as **kitten** is to **cat**

five is to **ten** as **eight** is to **sixteen**

Challenge Words

countenance (koun´ tə nəns)
foremost (fôr´ mōst)
nostalgia (nə stal´ jə)
orthodox (ôr´ thə doks)
vigilant (vij´ ə lənt)

■ **TEACHER TIP:** See page ix for suggestions on how to use this page.

WORDS IN CONTEXT

Read each sentence below to figure out the meaning of the word in **bold**. Use reasoning skills and the remainder of the sentence to help you. Write the meaning of the word on the line.

1. The **horde** of happy fans rushed the field and tore down the goalposts.

   <u>a swarm of people</u>

2. The detectives hoped new clues would **shed** light on the baffling crime.

   <u>to pour or send out</u>

3. Before Ryan returns to school, he will **recuperate** from the flu at home.

   <u>to get well</u>

4. A spider can **entangle** several small bugs in its web.

   <u>to wrap up or catch</u>

5. The **stir** caused by the president's arrival did not calm down for hours.

   <u>a great excitement</u>

6. The candidates continued to **debate** the issue of taxes until time ran out.

   <u>a discussion about a question or topic</u>

7. Alyssa was able to **manipulate** her brother into washing the car for her.

   <u>to control by clever use of unfair influence</u>

8. Our town's annual Kite Day provides a spectacular **aerial** display.

   <u>in or relating to the air</u>

9. Logan and Danielle negotiated an equal **division** of the weekend chores.

   <u>sharing some with each</u>

10. Our **perspective** from the mountaintop made the town below look small.

   <u>a view</u>

WORD MEANINGS

Word Learning

Study the spelling, part(s) of speech, and meaning(s) of each word. Complete each sentence by writing the word on the line. Then read the sentence.

1. **aerial** *(adj.)* in or relating to the air

   The _____**aerial**_____ display of the biplanes is my favorite part of the air show.

2. **blight** *(n.)* something that destroys or ruins

   The corn _____**blight**_____ is causing the farmers to have a poor crop this year.

3. **classification** *(n.)* arrangement into groups according to some system

   The _____**classification**_____ of books is determined by the Dewey decimal system.

4. **council** *(n.)* a gathering of people called together to give guidance and settle disagreements

   Neighborhood issues are discussed at meetings of the city _____**council**_____.

5. **debate** *(n.)* a discussion about a question or topic; *(v.)* 1. to discuss; 2. to talk about

   Ms. Lee's speech class held a _____**debate**_____ to discuss year-round classes.

   Cole and Christina _____**debate**_____ current events at the coffee shop.

6. **deter** *(v.)* to keep something from happening; 2. to prevent

   Snowfall is delaying airplanes and will _____**deter**_____ our arrival until tomorrow.

7. **division** *(n.)* 1. a separation; 2. sharing some with each

   If we assign a _____**division**_____ of tasks, we will get the job done quicker.

8. **entangle** *(v.)* 1. to wrap up or catch; 2. to interweave

   Mitchell learned to toss the fishing net so he wouldn't _____**entangle**_____ himself.

9. **generate** *(v.)* to create, produce, or make

   The circus manager is expecting the parade to _____**generate**_____ excitement.

10. **horde** *(n.)* 1. a swarm of people; 2. a crowd

    Times Square filled up with a _____**horde**_____ of people ready to celebrate the new year.

11. **inquire** *(v.)* to find out by asking questions

Let's _____ inquire _____ about the starting times for the new movie.

12. **manipulate** *(v.)* to control by clever use of unfair influence

The movie director can _____ manipulate _____ emotions with sad music.

13. **obstacle** *(n.)* something that stands in the way of progress

A fallen tree was one _____ obstacle _____ in Margaret's path.

14. **perspective** *(n.)* 1. a view; 2. a particular point of view

Today we can take a historical _____ perspective _____ on the events of 1963.

15. **precaution** *(n.)* concern taken in advance

As a _____ precaution _____, wear your seat belt when riding in a car.

16. **recuperate** *(v.)* 1. to get well; 2. to get back one's health or strength

It will take time to _____ recuperate _____ from your cold and get your energy back.

17. **shed** *(v.)* to pour or send out

She's not really sad; she is just able to _____ shed _____ tears easily.

18. **stir** *(v.)* 1. to strongly affect; 2. to excite or arouse; *(n.)* a great excitement

A double play is a sure way to _____ stir _____ the crowd's excitement.

Plans to build a mall created quite a _____ stir _____ in the village.

19. **valiant** *(adj.)* 1. brave; 2. bold; 3. fearless

The sheriff made a _____ valiant _____ effort to tame the Wild West town.

20. **wholesome** *(adj.)* 1. healthy; 2. good; 3. nutritious

A _____ wholesome _____ lunch might include whole wheat bread and fruit.

Vocabulary in Action

The words **council** and *counsel* are homophones. They are pronounced the same but have different spellings and meanings. A council is a gathering of people called together to give guidance and settle disagreements. It can also be an adjective that describes a noun, such as "the council chambers." A counsel is someone who gives advice. *Counsel* can also be a verb meaning "to advise." *Council* cannot be a verb. An easy way to remember the difference between the two words is to remember that the word with an *e* is generally one person.

Use Your Vocabulary

Choose the word from the Word List that best completes each sentence. Write the word on the line. You may use the plural form of nouns and the past tense of verbs if necessary.

Cows Run Amuck as Beetle Mania Sweeps Pasture

Liverpool, Wisconsin—Farmers are suffering a terrible **1** of shaggy-haired beetles. Yesterday, these winged, **2** bugs suddenly landed on rocks and rolled onto the cow pastures, making a guitar and drumlike noise. The usually contented cows **3** their common sense, screamed, and fainted. Legs and tails of swooning cows became **4**, making it difficult for rescue workers to sort out the cows. Farmers made a courageous and **5** effort to save their cows by carrying them into the barn.

"An event like this defies **6**," said the baffled governor. "It just doesn't fit into any known group of catastrophes."

The town **7** gathered to discuss the situation, and after a long **8**, they decided to take **9** to prevent a repeat visit by this invading **10** of beetles. A committee, searching for **11** to **12** insects from coming into this area, will share a **13** of labor to get to the bottom of the problem.

"The TV media is to blame for this," said the mayor. "They have **14** a frenzy of excitement, and the younger cows are easily **15** by clever journalists making something out of nothing."

Farmer Cynthia said, "What we need in this country is good, **16** bugs, not these shaggy ones. Someone should get out the scissors and do something about their appearance."

To get another **17**, this reporter approached a teen cow to **18** about her opinion. "I think the beetles are just groovy, don't you?" she said.

All overcome cows are expected to **19** as soon as the beetles move on. "We're playing classical music on the barn radios to **20** these cows back to producing milk, but so far the heifers aren't responding," said the president of the dairy council.

1. _____ blight
2. _____ aerial
3. _____ shed
4. _____ entangled
5. _____ valiant
6. _____ classification
7. _____ council
8. _____ debate
9. _____ precautions
10. _____ horde
11. _____ obstacles
12. _____ deter
13. _____ division
14. _____ generated
15. _____ manipulated
16. _____ wholesome
17. _____ perspective
18. _____ inquire
19. _____ recuperate
20. _____ stir

 **SYNONYMS**

Synonyms are words that have the same or nearly the same meanings.

Part 1 Choose the word from the box that is the best synonym for each group of words. Write the word on the line.

generate	stir	blight	inquire
precaution	shed	deter	wholesome

1. let flow, spill, give forth _____ shed _____

2. investigate, ask, explore _____ inquire _____

3. safety measure, protection, security _____ precaution _____

4. discourage, stop, impede _____ deter _____

5. good for you, healthful _____ wholesome _____

6. form, invent, originate _____ generate _____

7. disease, plague, destructive force _____ blight _____

8. energize; commotion, uproar _____ stir _____

Part 2 Replace the underlined word(s) with a word from the box that means the same or almost the same. Write your answer on the line.

horde	entangle	recuperate	council
division	obstacle	valiant	

9. Traffic was slowed down by the <u>barrier</u> in the road. _____ obstacle _____

10. A <u>mob</u> of autograph-seekers waited noisily at the stage door.
_____ horde _____

11. Diego would like to be elected to a position on the <u>board</u>. _____ council _____

12. Flying bats will not <u>ensnare</u> themselves in your hair. _____ entangle _____

13. Carter encouraged his soldiers with a <u>courageous</u> speech. _____ valiant _____

14. How long did it take you to <u>get better</u> after having the chicken pox?
_____ recuperate _____

15. The best part of having a lemonade stand is the <u>splitting up</u> of the profits.

_____division_____

 **ANTONYMS**

Antonyms are words that have opposite or nearly opposite meanings.

Part 1 Choose the word from the box that is the best antonym for each group of words. Write the word on the line.

inquire	valiant	generate	aerial	entangle

1. free, unravel _____entangle_____

2. cowardly, fearful, afraid _____valiant_____

3. reply, answer, respond _____inquire_____

4. grounded, of the earth _____aerial_____

5. stop making, destroy _____generate_____

Part 2 Replace the underlined word(s) with a word from the box that means the opposite or almost the opposite. Write your answer on the line.

shed	stir	recuperate	deter	wholesome

6. This school band knows how to <u>calm</u> the students before a big game.

_____stir_____

7. No health report can convince me that chocolate is really <u>harmful</u>.

_____wholesome_____

8. Trenton insisted that a real man will <u>hold back</u> his tears. _____shed_____

9. "I think you can expect to <u>worsen</u> in the next few days," said the doctor.

_____recuperate_____

10. A big fence will <u>encourage</u> everyone's plans to play in the park.

_____deter_____

WORD STUDY

Analogies To complete the following analogies, decide what kind of relationship is shown by the first pair of words. Then fill in the bubble next to the word that is the best choice for completing the second pair of words with the same relationship.

1. **scenic** is to **ugly** as **confident** is to _____

   (a.) smooth   (c.) anger

   (b.) nervous   (d.) view

2. **anger** is to **rage** as **adhere** is to _____

   (a.) loosen   **(c.)** attach

   (b.) joy   (d.) postage

3. **member** is to **council** as **player** is to _____

   (a.) coach   (c.) stadium

   (b.) fans   **(d.)** team

4. **pedestrian** is to **sidewalk** as **chauffeur** is to _____

   (a.) cement   (c.) uniforms

   (b.) limousine   (d.) passengers

5. **always** is to **never** as **many** is to _____

   (a.) forever   (c.) obscure

   (b.) much   **(d.)** none

CHALLENGE WORDS

Word Learning—Challenge!

Study the spelling, part(s) of speech, and meaning(s) of each word. Complete each sentence by writing the word on the line. Then read the sentence.

1. **countenance** *(n.)* a calm and approving expression; *(v.)* to offer approval or permission

   Alondra's calm smile gives her a pleasing _____countenance_____ .

   The committee will _____countenance_____ your plan to start a new club.

2. **foremost** *(adj.)* most important or first in a series of items

   Gerardo was our _____foremost_____ choice to receive the sportsmanship award.

3. **nostalgia** *(n.)* 1. sentimental yearning for a past period; 2. state of being homesick

   Serena feels _____nostalgia_____ for the days when movies were only a dollar.

4. **orthodox** *(adj.)* conforming to an established doctrine, such as a religious or political group

   To join our club, you must follow our _____orthodox_____ way of doing things.

5. **vigilant** *(adj.)* very alert and watchful

   A security guard needs to be an attentive, _____vigilant_____ person.

Use Your Vocabulary—Challenge!

An Artist's Plan Imagine that you are an artist planning a painting. Your painting will deal with farmers whose fields have been invaded by hordes of insects. Using the Challenge Words above, write a description of what you plan to paint. Be sure to describe the farmers' faces.

> ### Vocabulary in Action
>
> What do words beginning with *vig-*, such as ***vigilant***, *vigilante*, and *vigil*, have in common? For one thing, they all involve the act of watching. *Vigilant* means "very alert and watchful"; *vigilante* is from the Spanish word meaning "watchman" or "guard"; and one definition of *vigil* is "a watch kept on the night before a religious feast."

FUN WITH WORDS

Anagrams An anagram is a word made by mixing up the letters of one word in order to spell another word. For example, rearranging the letters of the word *moat* gives the anagram *atom*. The letters are the same; they're just in a different order.

In the activity below, you'll see an equation like this:

Example: hero + d = a lot of heroes _____horde_____

The letters to the left of the equal sign are an anagram of one of the vocabulary words (plus one or two additional letters that are needed to complete the vocabulary word). The words to the right of the equal sign give you a hint. In the sample above, combine the letters from the word *hero* with the letter *d* and rearrange them. You should come up with *horde*, which means "a lot of people." Write the vocabulary word in the blank.

1. tree + d = trying to stop a tree _____deter_____

2. liar + ae = a flying liar _____aerial_____

3. ed + beat = a formal discussion with Ed _____debate_____

4. coil + cun = a gathering of wise coils _____council_____

5. anvil + at = a brave iron block _____valiant_____

6. teen + ager = a kid wanting to create things _____generate_____

7. closet + ab = a closet that's in the way _____obstacle_____

8. creature + ep = a creature that's getting better _____recuperate_____

9. platinum + ae = this metal wants to control you _____manipulate_____

10. creepiest + vp = depends on how you look at it _____perspective_____

Review 7-9

Word Meanings Fill in the bubble of the word that is best defined by each phrase.

1. an assembly of people called together for advice
   - a. corridor
   - b. beacon
   - c. division
   - **d. council**

2. the power or strength to endure
   - a. perspective
   - **b. stamina**
   - c. blight
   - d. posterity

3. to move in a zigzag pattern
   - a. sprawl
   - **b. weave**
   - c. generate
   - d. manipulate

4. actual and precise
   - **a. literal**
   - b. serene
   - c. inevitable
   - d. urban

5. to engage in a formal argument
   - a. detect
   - b. correspond
   - **c. debate**
   - d. deter

6. a light used as a signal or warning
   - a. harbor
   - b. shaft
   - c. precaution
   - **d. beacon**

7. to do something in response
   - a. dissolve
   - b. stir
   - **c. react**
   - d. gasp

8. to surround and try to take
   - a. rebel
   - **b. besiege**
   - c. civilize
   - d. impede

9. having to do with the air
   - **a. aerial**
   - b. literal
   - c. advisable
   - d. wholesome

10. to influence with skill or cunning
    - a. pore
    - b. whisk
    - **c. manipulate**
    - d. distort

11. the act of giving attention to
    - a. classification
    - b. precaution
    - c. persuasion
    - **d. observation**

12. to keep from doing something
    - a. entangle
    - **b. deter**
    - c. detach
    - d. shed

13. the quality of being transparent
    - a. initiative
    - b. stamina
    - **c. clarity**
    - d. nonabrasive

14. to keep something going
    - **a. uphold**
    - b. inquire
    - c. enrage
    - d. civilize

15. something that is in the way
    - **a. obstacle**
    - b. pedestrian
    - c. blight
    - d. shaft

16. to slash or crush badly
    - **a. mangle**
    - b. enlist
    - c. entangle
    - d. detect

17. without definite size and shape
    - a. nonabrasive
    - b. valiant
    - c. adventurous
    - **d. gaseous**

18. to move with light, rapid strokes
    a. whisk   **b.** dissolve   **c.** distort   **d.** obscure

19. a large number of people
    a. pedestrian   **b.** timid   **c.** horde   **d.** clarity

20. to make someone extremely angry
    a. enlist   **b.** enrage   **c.** recuperate   **d.** shed

Sentence Completion
Choose the word from the box that best completes each of the following sentences. Write the word in the blank.

serene	stir	pores	recuperated	corridors
posterity	gasped	harbor	inquired	impede

1. The teacher _____ *inquired* _____ about my missing homework.

2. The _____ *pores* _____ on an elephant's skin can easily be seen by the unaided eye.

3. Once the ducks began to quack noisily, the _____ *serene* _____ moment ended.

4. Our family takes a formal photograph every year for _____ *posterity* _____.

5. Trying to _____ *impede* _____ Gary's rush to his bedroom is like trying to stop a train.

6. Julio _____ *gasped* _____ when I jumped out in front of him.

7. The mansion had so many different _____ *corridors* _____ that I soon became lost.

8. Natalia _____ *recuperated* _____ quickly from her bicycle accident.

9. The arrival of the parade floats caused quite a _____ *stir* _____.

10. Mom said we could _____ *harbor* _____ the stray cat, but only for a few days.

Fill in the Blanks
Fill in the bubble of the pair of words that best completes each sentence.

1. When Arturo said, "I'm hungry enough to eat a horse," his _____ younger brother was afraid he was being _____.
    a. valiant, inevitable   **c.** timid, literal
    b. enraged, advisable   **d.** adventurous, obscure

2. Some of the ideas the _____ brought up were too _____ for the voters to understand.

  a. pedestrian, timid   **c.** horde, inevitable

  b. council, obscure   **d.** rebel, valiant

3. It is _____ to eat a diet of _____ foods such as fruits, vegetables, and whole grains.

  a. advisable, wholesome   **c.** inevitable, serene

  b. adventurous, aerial   **d.** civilized, nonabrasive

4. If you _____ the doctor's help, you will _____ in no time at all.

  a. mangle, stir   **c.** enlist, recuperate

  b. deter, correspond   **d.** impede, whisk

5. The damaged ship sailed into the _____, skillfully avoiding all _____.

  a. corridor, observations   **c.** beacon, pedestrians

  b. division, shafts   **d.** harbor, obstacles

6. If you have _____ of vision and lots of _____, you will achieve your goals.

  a. clarity, stamina   **c.** perspective, blight

  b. posterity, pores   **d.** precaution, perspective

7. The _____ police officer dived into the _____ to save the little boy.

  a. timid, council   **c.** valiant, harbor

  b. urban, obstacle   **d.** adventurous, perspective

8. The _____ of buzzing bees _____ the bull.

  a. classification, detected   **c.** corridor, besieged

  b. horde, enraged   **d.** blight, distorted

9. It is _____ that rush hour traffic will _____ our progress.

  a. wholesome, manipulate   **c.** valiant, distort

  b. nonabrasive, weave   **d.** inevitable, impede

10. An audience member _____ about the subject of the _____.

  a. gasped, obstacle   **c.** dissolved, beacon

  b. inquired, debate   **d.** detected, rebel

Classifying Words Sort the words in the box by writing each word to complete a phrase in the correct category.

adventurous	aerial	beacon	council	harbor
horde	impede	observation	obstacles	pedestrians
perspective	persuasion	posterity	precaution	react
serene	stamina	timid	urban	wholesome

Words You Might Use to Talk About Outer Space

1. the moon shining like a(n) __beacon__ for the *Apollo* astronauts
2. a satellite whose purpose is the __observation__ of Mars
3. taking __aerial__ photos of the earth from a spaceship
4. leaving footsteps on the moon for __posterity__
5. taking every __precaution__ so our astronauts will be safe

Words You Might Use to Talk About Cities

6. stopping for __pedestrians__ in crosswalks
7. clearing the ice from the __harbor__ in winter
8. committees making plans for __urban__ renewal
9. being elected to the city __council__
10. making sure nothing will __impede__ ambulances

Words You Might Use to Talk About Business

11. having the __stamina__ to put in long hours
12. using __persuasion__ to convince customers to buy
13. overcoming __obstacles__ that stand in your way
14. being ready to __react__ quickly to trends in the market
15. not being too __timid__ to try out new ideas

Words You Might Use to Talk About Vacation

16. a(n) __horde__ of people crowding the beach
17. getting outdoors in the __wholesome__ fresh air
18. a(n) __adventurous__ ride down the river on a raft
19. seeing everything from a new __perspective__
20. feeling peaceful and __serene__

WORD LIST

Read each word using the pronunciation key.

ailment (āl´ mənt)
boisterous (boi´ stər əs)
coax (kōks)
cringe (krinj)
determination (di tər mə nā´ shən)
distraught (dis trôt´)
dual (dōō´ əl)
entrust (en trust´)
generator (jen´ ə rā tər)
humiliation (hyōō mil ē ā´ shən)
invigorate (in vig´ ə rāt)
marine (mə rēn´)
oddly (od´ lē)
parallel (pâr´ ə lel)
presume (pri zōōm´)
relations (ri lā´ shənz)
shrill (shril)
strenuous (stren´ yōō əs)
variable (vâr´ ē ə bəl)
wistful (wist´ fəl)

WORD STUDY

Prefixes

The prefix *fore-* means "in front or before."

forecast (fôr´ kast) *(n.)* a statement of what is coming
forefather (fôr´ fä thər) *(n.)* an ancestor
forepaw (fôr´ pô) *(n.)* a front paw
foresee (fôr sē´) *(v.)* to know beforehand
foresight (fôr´ sīt) *(n.)* the power to know beforehand
foretell (fôr tel´) *(v.)* to predict

Challenge Words

detest (di test´)
fruitless (frōōt´ ləs)
haggle (hag´ əl)
patronize (pā´ trə nīz)
procure (prō kyŏor´)

■ **TEACHER TIP:** See page ix for suggestions on how to use this page.   *Level F*

WORDS IN CONTEXT

Read each sentence below to figure out the meaning of the word in **bold**. Use reasoning skills and the remainder of the sentence to help you. Write the meaning of the word on the line.

1. An **ailment**, such as the common cold, is unpleasant but not fatal.

   a sickness or an illness

2. The bus driver asked the **boisterous** football team to quiet down.

   cheerfully loud

3. Since Austin is so responsible, I will **entrust** him with the money we collected.

   to turn something over to someone else's care

4. The ice-cream store has a backup **generator** in case the electricity goes out.

   a machine used to make electricity from mechanical energy

5. Lauren saw crabs, sea stars, and other **marine** life at the seashore aquarium.

   of or found in the sea

6. If you are weary, a day of hiking in the fresh mountain air will **invigorate** you.

   to fill with energy and life

7. Courtney had the **determination** she needed to finish this year's marathon.

   having great purpose

8. In preparation for the graduation, chairs were set up in neat, **parallel** rows.

   the same distance apart at every point

9. Mary tried to **coax** her sister to the party by saying how much fun it would be.

   to influence or persuade by using kindness

10. Griffin let out a **shrill** scream when Brian surprised him.

    having a sharp, high pitch or sound

WORD MEANINGS

Word Learning

Study the spelling, part(s) of speech, and meaning(s) of each word. Complete each sentence by writing the word on the line. Then read the sentence.

1. **ailment** *(n.)* a sickness or an illness

   What _____<u>ailment</u>_____ is keeping you home from school today?

2. **boisterous** *(adj.)* cheerfully loud

   Nothing is as noisy as a _____<u>boisterous</u>_____ three-year-old on her birthday.

3. **coax** *(v.)* to influence or persuade by using kindness

   Promise him anything, but you will never _____<u>coax</u>_____ Chase to eat spinach.

4. **cringe** *(v.)* to shrink in fear, pain, or danger

   The lion's ferocious roar caused the kindergartners to _____<u>cringe</u>_____.

5. **determination** *(n.)* having great purpose

   The athletes ran around the last bend with great _____<u>determination</u>_____.

6. **distraught** *(adj.)* irrational; upset

   Faith, _____<u>distraught</u>_____ over losing her key, sat on the steps and cried.

7. **dual** *(adj.)* made up of two parts

   Instead of playing only one role, every actor had _____<u>dual</u>_____ roles in the play.

8. **entrust** *(v.)* to turn something over to someone else's care

   I _____<u>entrust</u>_____ my best friend with my most private thoughts.

9. **generator** *(n.)* a machine used to make electricity from mechanical energy

   Let's start the _____<u>generator</u>_____ and get the baseball field lit up.

10. **humiliation** *(n.)* a lowering of self-respect

    I felt such _____<u>humiliation</u>_____ when I tripped over the tree branch.

11. **invigorate** *(v.)* to fill with energy and life

    Does playing a soccer game _____<u>invigorate</u>_____ you or tire you out?

12. **marine** *(adj.)* 1. of or found in the sea; 2. produced by the sea; *(n.)* a person serving in the United States Marine Corps (usually Marine)

An oil spill in the ocean affects the _____ marine _____ life.

My grandfather was a _____ Marine _____ in World War II.

13. **oddly** *(adv.)* 1. in a peculiar or an unusual manner; 2. weirdly

Jazmin walks _____ oddly _____ when she wears her snow boots.

14. **parallel** *(adj.)* 1. the same distance apart at every point; 2. similar

The _____ parallel _____ streets of Heather and Poplar are the east and west boundaries.

15. **presume** *(v.)* 1. to assume; 2. to take for granted

The judge told the jury to _____ presume _____ the defendant's innocence.

16. **relations** *(n.)* the connection or association between persons, groups, or countries

Tourism increased when _____ relations _____ improved between the countries.

17. **shrill** *(adj.)* having a sharp, high pitch or sound

Maya directs her sheep with a _____ shrill _____, high-pitched whistle.

18. **strenuous** *(adj.)* 1. very forceful; 2. active

Running, swimming, and cycling are _____ strenuous _____ exercise.

19. **variable** *(adj.)* 1. changeable; 2. uncertain; *(n.)* something that is likely to change

You'll hear _____ variable _____ amounts of noise from each classroom.

We don't know who is coming, so it is a _____ variable _____ in our plans.

20. **wistful** *(adj.)* 1. longing; 2. yearning

Julian looked into the bakery window with a _____ wistful _____ expression.

Vocabulary in Action

What is the difference between **determination** and *persistence*? Read the following quote from Calvin Coolidge and see if you are persistent enough to determine the subtle difference between the two words.

"Nothing in the world can take the place of persistence. Talent will not; nothing is more common than unsuccessful men with talent. Genius will not; unrewarded genius is almost a proverb. Education will not; the world is full of educated derelicts. Persistence and determination alone are omnipotent. The slogan 'Press On' has solved and always will solve the problems of the human race."

—Calvin Coolidge (1872–1933), 30th president of United States

Use Your Vocabulary

Choose the word from the Word List that best completes each sentence. Write the word on the line. You may use the plural form of nouns and the past tense of verbs if necessary.

To help build good __1__ between our community and those who serve it, a park ranger visited our class. He spoke enthusiastically about the variety of __2__ life found along the shores of our state. The ranger explained that the number of tourists visiting our beaches was __3__ from season to season.

    The ranger answered questions about the ocean and shore environment, but he __4__ when someone asked about the effect of oil spills. He seemed __5__ when he told us that he worries about the harm caused by such spills. For example, he told us that chemicals and oil in the water have caused a number of serious __6__ in birds and other shore animals. The ranger said, "The care of our planet has been __7__ to us, so we should try to keep the earth clean and healthy."

    In a(n) __8__ voice, he spoke of his desire to stroll on a clean beach. "I want our beach to be a source of pride and not __9__, so I've organized a beach cleanup day," the ranger said. "May I __10__ that everyone will join our cleanup efforts?" He did not need to __11__ us to join. We were eager to help.

    On cleanup day, we approached the task with __12__. We organized ourselves into __13__ lines across the beach to thoroughly cover the area. Then we walked along, picking up litter and putting it in a bag. It was enjoyable, and not at all __14__ work. In fact, the cool breeze helped __15__ us. The __16__ cries of the seagulls flying overhead reminded us that we were helping many animals.

    What a(n) __17__ group we were, laughing and chatting as we picked up trash. We were so purposeful that no one goofed off or behaved __18__. We stopped at dusk but would have continued if we had had an electrical __19__ to provide energy for the lights. Our work served a(n) __20__ purpose: We both cleaned up our beach and made a new friend.

1. _____ relations _____
2. _____ marine _____
3. _____ variable _____
4. _____ cringed _____
5. _____ distraught _____
6. _____ ailments _____
7. _____ entrusted _____
8. _____ wistful _____
9. _____ humiliation _____
10. _____ presume _____
11. _____ coax _____
12. _____ determination _____
13. _____ parallel _____
14. _____ strenuous _____
15. _____ invigorate _____
16. _____ shrill _____
17. _____ boisterous _____
18. _____ oddly _____
19. _____ generator _____
20. _____ dual _____

SYNONYMS

Synonyms are words that have the same or nearly the same meanings.

Part 1 Choose the word from the box that is the best synonym for each group of words. Write the word on the line.

ailment	**oddly**	**wistful**	**entrust**
strenuous	**coax**	**variable**	**humiliation**

1. strangely, irregularly _____ oddly

2. convince, urge, encourage _____ coax

3. disease, disorder, complaint _____ ailment

4. changeable; alterable _____ variable

5. embarrassment, unease, shame _____ humiliation

6. energetic, active _____ strenuous

7. charge with, assign, give to _____ entrust

8. hopeful, wishing for, thoughtful _____ wistful

Part 2 Replace the underlined word(s) with a word from the box that means the same or almost the same. Write your answer on the line.

distraught	**determination**	**presume**	**dual**
boisterous	**relations**	**invigorate**	

9. Lillian pounded on the podium and spoke with <u>firmness</u>. _____ determination

10. Eating breakfast will <u>energize</u> you for the day ahead. _____ invigorate

11. The <u>worried</u> look on Dan's face told us something was wrong.
_____ distraught

12. Some <u>noisy, rowdy</u> boys rushed onto the field. _____ boisterous

13. With twins, parents have to get <u>double</u> strollers. _____ dual

14. <u>Personal connections</u> between us have never been better. _____ Relations

15. When the two explorers met, one said to the other, "Dr. Livingston, I <u>conclude</u>?"

_____ presume _____

ANTONYMS

Antonyms are words that have opposite or nearly opposite meanings.

Part 1 Choose the word from the box that is the best antonym for each group of words. Write the word on the line.

coax	**oddly**	**variable**
distraught	**entrust**	**shrill**

1. normally, in a familiar way   _____ oddly _____

2. discourage, deter, curb   _____ coax _____

3. stable, predictable; constant   _____ variable _____

4. withdraw, withhold, refuse   _____ entrust _____

5. having a low-pitched, quiet sound   _____ shrill _____

6. comfortable, happy, at peace   _____ distraught _____

Part 2 Replace the underlined word(s) with a word from the box that means the opposite or almost the opposite. Write your answer on the line.

humiliation	parallel	invigorate	strenuous	relations

7. There is a committee investigating the <u>lack of contact</u> between the two rival schools. _____ relations _____

8. Kai needs an <u>effortless</u> activity to occupy her after school. _____ strenuous _____

9. Hayden thinks a half hour on the exercise machines will <u>weaken</u> him.
_____ invigorate _____

10. That hat will only bring you <u>a rise in the opinion of yourself.</u>
_____ humiliation _____

11. The triplets were living <u>different</u> lives in different cities. _____ parallel _____

WORD STUDY

Prefixes Add the prefix *fore-* to these words. Then use each new word in a sentence.

1. cast _____forecast_____

_____Sentences will vary._____

_____

2. father _____forefather_____

_____

_____

3. paw _____forepaw_____

_____

_____

4. see _____foresee_____

_____

_____

5. sight _____foresight_____

_____

_____

6. tell _____foretell_____

_____

_____

CHALLENGE WORDS

Word Learning—Challenge!

Study the spelling, part of speech, and meaning(s) of each word. Complete each sentence by writing the word on the line. Then read the sentence.

1. **detest** *(v.)* 1. to feel great dislike for; 2. to hate

   "I _____detest_____ cold weather," said Kara, who used to live in Florida.

2. **fruitless** *(adj.)* 1. lacking fruit; 2. not successful

   Brooklyn remained cold after a _____fruitless_____ search for her jacket.

3. **haggle** *(v.)* 1. to bargain; 2. to argue in an attempt to come to an agreement

   You can _____haggle_____ at the village markets to get the best prices.

4. **patronize** *(v.)* 1. to provide frequent support for; 2. to treat condescendingly

   "Madam," said the chauffeur, "I do not like it when you _____patronize_____ me."

5. **procure** *(v.)* to attain with care and effort

   If you would like to sit down, I will _____procure_____ a chair for you.

Use Your Vocabulary—Challenge!

The Daily News You work for a newspaper. Your job is to write an editorial on a local environmental issue, using the Challenge Words above. On a separate sheet of paper, explain the problem, give your opinion, and suggest what your readers can do to help solve the problem. Try to persuade your readers to agree with you.

> ### Notable Quotes
>
> "If the study of all these sciences which we have enumerated should ever bring us to their mutual association and relationship, and teach us the nature of the ties which bind them together, I believe that the diligent treatment of them will forward the objects which we have in view, and that the labor, which otherwise would be **fruitless**, will be well bestowed."
>
> —Plato (428–348 BC), Greek philosopher

FUN WITH WORDS

Choose six of the following eight words. Write a paragraph in which you use the words to describe someone you know.

| boisterous | coax | determination | entrust |
| invigorate | presume | oddly | wistful |

Answers will vary.

_____

_____

_____

_____

_____

_____

_____

_____

_____

_____

_____

_____

_____

_____

_____

_____

_____

WORD LIST

Read each word using the pronunciation key.

ajar (ə jär´)
bombard (bom bärd´)
bough (bou)
collaborate (kə lab´ ə rāt)
criticism (krit´ i siz əm)
diameter (dī am´ i tər)
duplicate (*n., adj.* dōō´pli kit) (*v.* dōō pli kāt)
epidemic (ep i dem´ ik)
geologist (jē ol´ ə jist)
hustle (hus´ əl)
invalid (in val´ id)
irrational (i rash´ ə nəl)
maul (môl)
ointment (oint´ mənt)
prevail (pre vāl´)
reliance (re lī´ əns)
signify (sig´ nə fī)
stupefy (stōō´ pə fī)
variation (vâr ē ā´ shən)
wondrous (wun´ drəs)

WORD STUDY

Suffixes

The suffix *-ous* means "full of" or "having much."

courageous (kə rā´ jəs) *(adj.)* brave
dangerous (dān´ jər əs) *(adj.)* not safe
humorous (hyü´ mər əs) *(adj.)* funny
joyous (joi´ əs) *(adj.)* joyful, glad
ridiculous (ri dik´ yə ləs) *(adj.)* laughable
suspicious (sə spish´ əs) *(adj.)* questionable

Challenge Words

diminish (di min´ ish)
goad (gōd)
heed (hēd)
insistent (in sis´ tənt)
oppress (ə pres´)

TEACHER TIP: See page ix for suggestions on how to use this page.

Level F

WORDS IN CONTEXT

Read each sentence below to figure out the meaning of the word in **bold**. Use reasoning skills and the remainder of the sentence to help you. Write the meaning of the word on the line.

1. We'll really have to **hustle** to get to the movie on time.

   to hurry or move quickly

2. Please leave the door **ajar** so I can hear the baby if she cries.

   partially open

3. Will the three of you **collaborate** to finish the science project?

   to work cooperatively with others

4. Mrs. Post showed her **reliance** on me by appointing me to be fire marshal.

   trust; faith; confidence

5. I put my name on the petition to **signify** my agreement.

   to indicate by signs, words, or actions

6. The colors and grandeur of the Grand Canyon are a **wondrous** sight.

   wonderful

7. An **epidemic** of measles spread through several cities.

   quick spreading of a disease affecting many people at the same time

8. I will make a **duplicate** of the story I wrote in case I lose the original.

   a copy

9. The company's **geologist** studies the earth's crust to help find oil.

   an expert in the science of the earth's structure and history

10. The construction worker used a **maul** to drive the heavy stakes into the ground.

    a heavy hammer or mallet

WORD MEANINGS

Word Learning

Study the spelling, part(s) of speech, and meaning(s) of each word. Complete each sentence by writing the word on the line. Then read the sentence.

1. **ajar** *(adj.)* partially open

   Kayla left the basement door _____ajar_____ so the cat could come in.

2. **bombard** *(v.)* to continually attack with great force

   The press will _____bombard_____ the police chief with questions.

3. **bough** *(n.)* a branch of a tree

   The tree surgeon needed a ladder and a saw to trim the top _____bough_____.

4. **collaborate** *(v.)* to work cooperatively with others

   Five or six students can _____collaborate_____ to finish their assignments.

5. **criticism** *(n.)* negative statements or opinions

   That actor never reads reviews because he is sensitive to _____criticism_____.

6. **diameter** *(n.)* 1. a straight line that runs through the center of a circle or sphere; 2. the width or thickness of something that is circular

   This pipe has an opening that is six inches in _____diameter_____.

7. **duplicate** *(n.)* a copy, clone, or double; *(adj.)* exactly the same as something else; *(v.)* 1. to copy something exactly; 2. to reproduce

   Can you tell which is the _____duplicate_____ and which is the original?

   The sisters bought _____duplicate_____ sweatshirts.

   The sculptor was commissioned to _____duplicate_____ the original statue.

8. **epidemic** *(n.)* the quick spreading of a disease that affects many people at once

   In the nineteenth century, an outbreak of flu was a dangerous

   _____epidemic_____.

9. **geologist** *(n.)* an expert in the science of the earth's structure and history

   A _____geologist_____ spoke to our science class about the earth's formation.

10. **hustle** (v.) to hurry or move quickly; (n.) hurried action or motion

Brianna was late for dinner and had to _____ hustle _____ to be on time.

Trains and traffic add to the _____ hustle _____ and bustle of the big city.

11. **invalid** (adj.) 1. not true; 2. not sound

Due to a lack of information, William made an _____ invalid _____ decision.

12. **irrational** (adj.) not sensible or reasonable

There is no explanation for Adam's _____ irrational _____ behavior.

13. **maul** (n.) a heavy hammer or mallet; (v.) to beat or handle roughly

Abe Lincoln used a _____ maul _____ and a wedge to split logs.

Keep the cat away so she won't _____ maul _____ the fragile material.

14. **ointment** (n.) a greasy substance used to heal the skin or to make it soft

Apply this _____ ointment _____ to the cut on your hand to help it heal.

15. **prevail** (v.) to succeed or win

We expect last year's winner to _____ prevail _____ again in the tournament.

16. **reliance** (n.) trust; faith; confidence

Cody's _____ reliance _____ on the old car keeps him from getting a new one.

17. **signify** (v.) to indicate by signs, words, or actions

This card will _____ signify _____ your membership and admit you to the club.

18. **stupefy** (v.) 1. to stun or dull the senses of; 2. to amaze

The amazing circus high-wire act will _____ stupefy _____ you.

19. **variation** (n.) 1. a change; 2. a different form

A cold day on the equator is a _____ variation _____ in the normal weather.

20. **wondrous** (adj.) wonderful

The entire graduating class in caps and gowns is a _____ wondrous _____ sight.

Vocabulary in Action

Stupefy is a transitive verb derived from the Middle English word *stupifien.* This was a modification of the Latin word *stupefacere,* a combination of *stupere* ("to be astonished") and *facere* ("to make"). The origins of the word can be traced back to the 15th century.

Use Your Vocabulary

Choose the word from the Word List that best completes each sentence. Write the word on the line. You may use the plural form of nouns and the past tense of verbs if necessary.

My Aunt Dora, a(n) __1__ and athletic rock climber, invited me to go rock climbing with her. At first, I thought this was a(n) __2__ idea because I had already planned to spend my summer mowing lawns to earn extra money. Aunt Dora said she would not accept my __3__ excuses. She said I could mow lawns any summer, but how often would I get invited to go rock climbing? She said that she would leave the door of opportunity __4__, but I would be sorry if I did not take advantage of her offer. Aunt Dora thinks that nothing short of a deadly __5__ should keep a person from climbing rocks in the great outdoors. She continued to __6__ me with reasons as to why I should go until she __7__, and I agreed.

I had very little rock-climbing experience, so my __8__ on Aunt Dora's expertise was great. She encouraged me gently, not being one to give harsh __9__. She was patient as she showed me simple climbing techniques, but she saved the more difficult __10__ for herself. She would __11__ me with her __12__ climbing ability as she leaped from ledge to ledge with grace and skill.

We had to __13__ to solve any climbing problem. We had to cross a deep gully by swinging from a low __14__ of a nearby tree. First, Aunt Dora carefully estimated the __15__ of the branch to make sure it was thick enough to hold our weight. Then she swung over. I waved to her to __16__ that I was ready to cross. But when I tried to __17__ her graceful movements, I was not quite so successful. I landed clumsily and yelped in pain, thinking I had __18__ my leg. Aunt Dora calmly examined me and said I had only scratched my ankle. She applied a(n) __19__ that eased the sting of my wound. Next summer I'd rather __20__ behind the lawn mower than swing down a canyon wall.

1. _____ geologist
2. _____ irrational
3. _____ invalid
4. _____ ajar
5. _____ epidemic
6. _____ bombard
7. _____ prevailed
8. _____ reliance
9. _____ criticism
10. _____ variations
11. _____ stupefy
12. _____ wondrous
13. _____ collaborate
14. _____ bough
15. _____ diameter
16. _____ signify
17. _____ duplicate
18. _____ mauled
19. _____ ointment
20. _____ hustle

SYNONYMS

Synonyms are words that have the same or nearly the same meanings.

Part 1 Choose the word from the box that is the best synonym for each group of words. Write the word on the line.

criticism	ointment	bough	prevail
epidemic	variation	reliance	bombard

1. salve, balm, lotion   ointment

2. alteration, deviation, difference   variation

3. blitz, assault, charge   bombard

4. outbreak, plague   epidemic

5. limb, shoot   bough

6. triumph, achieve victory   prevail

7. disapproving comment   criticism

8. dependence, assurance, certainty   reliance

Part 2 Replace the underlined word with a word from the box that means the same or almost the same. Write your answer on the line.

stupefy	wondrous	invalid	hustle
irrational	signify	maul	

9. The protesters say it is <u>senseless</u> to cut down old elm trees just to widen a road.
   _____irrational_____

10. At an auction, you can <u>communicate</u> your bid with just a nod of your head.
    _____signify_____

11. To keep our pig from chewing shoes, we give him a rawhide toy to <u>mangle</u> instead. _____maul_____

12. "Our game strategy," said Juan, "will be to <u>rush</u> the other team's quarterback."
    _____hustle_____

13. The noisy arrival of the old airplanes will <u>astonish</u> the folks on the ground. _____*stupefy*_____

14. You'll need tickets if you want to hear our <u>marvelous</u> symphony orchestra. _____*wondrous*_____

15. Please correct any <u>false</u> information on your student identification. _____*invalid*_____

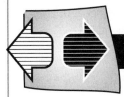 **ANTONYMS**

Antonyms are words that have opposite or nearly opposite meanings.

Part 1 Choose the word from the box that is the best antonym for each group of words. Write the word on the line.

prevail	irrational	collaborate	ajar	reliance

1. closed, shut, blocked _____*ajar*_____

2. work independently _____*collaborate*_____

3. fail, lose, be defeated _____*prevail*_____

4. doubt, misgiving, suspicion _____*reliance*_____

5. showing good judgment _____*irrational*_____

> ### Notable Quotes
>
> "We allow our ignorance to **prevail** upon us and make us think we can survive alone, alone in patches, alone in groups, alone in races, even alone in genders."
>
> —Maya Angelou (1928–), author, civil rights activist

Part 2 Replace the underlined word with a word from the box that means the opposite or almost the opposite. Write your answer on the line.

> criticism   variation   duplicate   wondrous   hustle

6. Brooke and Jordan always <u>dawdle</u> to class together. _____ hustle _____

7. Dakota's photographs told a story of a very <u>ordinary</u> vacation.
   _____ wondrous _____

8. Make a copy of your story on the copy machine and then give me the <u>original</u>.
   _____ duplicate _____

9. The <u>similarity</u> among the sweaters made it difficult to choose which one to wear.
   _____ variation _____

10. The dancers held their breath as they waited to hear their instructor's <u>praise</u>.
   _____ criticism _____

WORD STUDY

Suffixes Write the word from the box that has the same meaning as the first word and the suffix -*ous*.

> courageous   humorous   ridiculous
> dangerous   joyous   suspicious

1. chance of harm + ous = _____ dangerous _____

2. doubt + ous = _____ suspicious _____

3. gladness + ous = _____ joyous _____

4. bravery + ous = _____ courageous _____

5. make fun of + ous = _____ ridiculous _____

6. funny + ous = _____ humorous _____

CHALLENGE WORDS

Word Learning—Challenge!

Study the spelling, part(s) of speech, and meaning(s) of each word. Complete each sentence by writing the word on the line. Then read the sentence.

1. **diminish** *(v.)* 1. to decrease or make less; 2. to dwindle

    We waited for the rain to _____diminish_____ so we wouldn't get wet.

2. **goad** *(n.)* something that urges someone into action; *(v.)* to urge into action

    Ranchers use a _____goad_____, a pointed stick, to drive cattle on.

    Asking for money over the phone might _____goad_____ people into donating.

3. **heed** *(v.)* to pay attention to

    If you don't _____heed_____ my advice, you'll be making a mistake.

4. **insistent** *(adj.)* 1. holds attention; 2. persistent

    The _____insistent_____ dog refused to stop barking until it got its food.

5. **oppress** *(v.)* 1. to crush or burden by abusing power; 2. to burden physically or spiritually by abusing power

    A dictator can _____oppress_____ people by taking away their rights.

Use Your Vocabulary—Challenge!

Thank You Very Much Imagine that a favorite friend or relative has taken you along on an adventurous journey. On a separate sheet of paper, write a thank-you note to this person, using the Challenge Words above. Be sure to describe where the journey took place and what happened along the way.

> ### *Vocabulary in Action*
>
> The word ***wondrous*** is an adjective that comes from the word *wonder.* There are many synonyms for wondrous, including amazing, astonishing, astounding, fantastic, fantastical, incredible, marvelous, miraculous, phenomenal, prodigious, stupendous, and unbelievable.

Study the word web. Complete the sentences with vocabulary words from this chapter. Then write a paragraph about a problem you have solved.

Don't _____hustle_____. Slow down and think things through.

_____Signify_____ to others that you are working on improving the situation.

_____Collaborate_____ with others to find a solution.

Try to learn something from others' _____criticism_____.

Ways to Deal with Difficulties

_____Duplicate_____ actions that have worked in the past.

Be patient as you continue your efforts and you will _____prevail_____.

Try not to be _____irrational_____, even if you're angry.

_____Reliance_____ on yourself is good, but don't be bossy.

Vocabulary in Action

Heed can be used as an intransitive verb meaning "to pay attention to" or a transitive verb that means "to give consideration or attention to." The word is from the Middle and Old English *hedan,* which is similar to the Old High German *huota,* meaning "guard."

WORD LIST

Read each word using the pronunciation key.

acknowledge (ak nol´ ij)
alibi (al´ ə bī)
bore (bôr)
commemorate (kə mem´ ə rāt)
debut (dā byoo´)
digestion (dī jes´ chən)
drought (drout)
duration (doo rā´ shən)
erupt (i rupt´)
gloat (glōt)
hypocrite (hip´ ə krit)
irregular (i reg´ yə lər)
mental (men´ təl)
oracle (ôr´ ə kəl)
prevention (pre ven´ shən)
reservoir (rez´ ər vwär)
simmer (sim´ ər)
sturdy (stər´ dē)
vast (vast)
wrangle (raŋ´ gəl)

WORD STUDY

Prefixes

The prefix *over-* means "beyond" or "too much."

overcharge (ō vər charj´) *(v.)* to charge too much
overcooked (ō vər kükt´) *(adj.)* cooked too much
overflow (ō vər flō´) *(v.)* to cover or flood
overload (ō vər lōd´) *(v.)* to load too heavily
overpay (ō vər pā´) *(v.)* to pay too much
oversleep (ō vər slēp´) *(v.)* to sleep beyond the time for waking

Challenge Words

elongate (ē loŋ´ gāt)
indispenable (in di spens´ ə bəl)
lubricate (loo´ bri kāt)
pending (pen´ diŋ)
unscathed (un skāt̸hd´)

■ **TEACHER TIP:** See page ix for suggestions on how to use this page.

Read each sentence below to figure out the meaning of the word in **bold**. Use reasoning skills and the remainder of the sentence to help you. Write the meaning of the word on the line.

1. The statue of Albert Einstein will **commemorate** his great contributions to physics.

   to honor the memory of

2. What **prevention** can you take to keep accidents from happening in your home?

   a keeping from happening

3. This recipe says that tomato sauce should **simmer** over low heat for two hours.

   to keep the temperature just below the boiling point

4. John can be a **bore** when he tells long, dull stories about his job.

   a wearisome, dull person

5. Several witnesses back up David's **alibi** that he was at home at nine o'clock.

   a statement by an accused person claiming to be elsewhere when a crime was committed

6. I've been anxiously awaiting the **debut** of the new mystery series on TV.

   the first presentation of someone or something

7. Much of the southwestern United States is a grand, **vast** desert area.

   extremely large

8. If we don't get rain soon, this summer will be officially declared a **drought**.

   a period of dryness

9. Many ancient plays speak of an **oracle** who could predict future events.

   a person through which a god is believed to speak

10. Scientists can often give a warning as to when a volcano will **erupt**.

    to explode with great force

WORD MEANINGS

Word Learning

Study the spelling, part(s) of speech, and meaning(s) of each word. Complete each sentence by writing the word on the line. Then read the sentence.

1. **acknowledge** *(v.)* 1. to recognize; 2. to admit; 3. to concede

   Zachary's parents were happy to hear him _____acknowledge_____ his guilt.

2. **alibi** *(n.)* 1. a statement from an accused person claiming to be elsewhere when a crime was committed; 2. an excuse

   The burglar had an airtight _____alibi_____, so the police let him go.

3. **bore** *(n.)* a wearisome, dull person or thing; *(v.)* to make a hole by pushing, twisting, or digging

   The movie was a _____bore_____, so we left halfway through it.

   The carpenter used a drill to _____bore_____ a peephole into the front door.

4. **commemorate** *(v.)* to honor the memory of someone or something

   The memorial service will _____commemorate_____ the late mayor's life.

5. **debut** *(n.)* the first presentation of someone or something; *(v.)* to make a first appearance

   All of Anthony's family and friends came to see his acting _____debut_____.

   The new play will _____debut_____ at an off-Broadway theater.

6. **digestion** *(n.)* the process in which food is changed in the stomach and intestines so that the body can use it

   Exercise and healthy eating will promote good _____digestion_____.

7. **drought** *(n.)* 1. a period of dryness; 2. a long time without rain

   The farmers are irrigating to help the crops survive the _____drought_____.

8. **duration** *(n.)* the length of time in which something occurs

   The _____duration_____ of the school year is about nine months.

9. **erupt** *(v.)* to explode with great force

   Geologists want to know what caused the volcano to _____erupt_____.

10. **gloat** *(v.)* to think with pleasure about something unfortunate that happened to someone else or good that happened to oneself

It's impolite to _____ gloat _____, even if you did beat your opponent.

11. **hypocrite** *(n.)* a person who expresses feelings or beliefs that he or she really doesn't believe in

The candidate was accused of being a _____ hypocrite _____ because he voted for a law he once opposed.

12. **irregular** *(adj.)* 1. not being or acting according to rule; 2. out of normal order; 3. uneven

The floor tiles were placed in an unusual, _____ irregular _____ pattern.

13. **mental** *(adj.)* 1. of or by the mind; 2. having an illness of the mind

This hospital is for patients suffering from _____ mental _____ confusion.

14. **oracle** *(n.)* a person through which a god is believed to speak

It was believed that the _____ oracle _____ at Delphi spoke wisely.

15. **prevention** *(n.)* 1. a keeping from happening; 2. a hindering

Our local firefighter talked to us about fire _____ prevention _____.

16. **reservoir** *(n.)* a place where water is stored for future use

The dam creates a _____ reservoir _____ that supplies water to the desert.

17. **simmer** *(v.)* to keep the temperature just below the boiling point

Turn the burner to low and _____ simmer _____ the stew in the pot.

18. **sturdy** *(adj.)* 1. strong; 2. well-built

With seven boys in the family, the Olsens need _____ sturdy _____ furniture.

19. **vast** *(adj.)* 1. extremely large; 2. immense

To cross Russia, you will cover a _____ vast _____ distance by train.

20. **wrangle** *(v.)* to quarrel in a noisy or an angry way

The boys always _____ wrangle _____ over who will play the video game next.

Vocabulary in Action

The word **mental** comes from the Latin root *mens,* which means "mind." Other words with the same root are *mention, mentality, and mentation.*

Use Your Vocabulary

Choose the word from the Word List that best completes each sentence. Write the word on the line. You may use the plural form of nouns and the past tense of verbs if necessary.

Memorial Day is a holiday to __1__ all those in the armed services who served our country. Although Memorial Day is a serious, important event, it's still fun and not a(n) __2__ in our town. Our mayor gave a speech of about 15 minutes in __3__. He gratefully __4__ the sacrifices made by so many people to preserve liberty in this country. His description of his experiences as a soldier gave me a clear __5__ picture of the Vietnam War.

This celebration was particularly special, as our new town chorus made its singing __6__. The crowd __7__ into applause. Then the big town picnic was held at the __8__. It was pleasant near the human-made lake, even though the recent __9__ has kept the water level too low for boating. Everyone brought a special dish to share, so we ended up with __10__ amounts of different foods to enjoy. People ate as much as their __11__ could handle. Everyone looked forward to Mrs. King's baked beans. She likes to __12__ the beans on the stove and tease us with the wonderful smell long before the picnic. Adults and kids jokingly pushed one another and __13__ to be the first in line for Mrs. King's beans.

I sat on a lawn chair that was not too __14__ and ended up on the ground with a plateful of food in my lap. I think my brother had something to do with it, but he claimed to have a(n) __15__ about being in the food line when the chair collapsed. He showed great concern for my well-being, but I think he was being a(n) __16__, because later I heard him __17__ over how silly I looked with my dinner all over me. I'm not surprised. It would be __18__ if my brother did not play a trick on me.

It was pretty much a perfect day except for the weather. If we had a(n) __19__ who could accurately tell us the weather, we might have brought jackets as a(n) __20__ against being uncomfortable in the cold.

1. _____ commemorate _____
2. _____ bore _____
3. _____ duration _____
4. _____ acknowledged _____
5. _____ mental _____
6. _____ debut _____
7. _____ erupted _____
8. _____ reservoir _____
9. _____ drought _____
10. _____ vast _____
11. _____ digestion _____
12. _____ simmer _____
13. _____ wrangled _____
14. _____ sturdy _____
15. _____ alibi _____
16. _____ hypocrite _____
17. _____ gloat _____
18. _____ irregular _____
19. _____ oracle _____
20. _____ prevention _____

SYNONYMS

Synonyms are words that have the same or nearly the same meanings.

Part 1 Choose the word from the box that is the best synonym for each group of words. Write the word on the line.

| simmer | hypocrite | erupt | commemorate |
| prevention | sturdy | bore | acknowledge |

1. stopping, deterrence _____ prevention _____

2. confess, own up to, confirm _____ acknowledge _____

3. solid, rugged, hearty _____ sturdy _____

4. pay tribute to _____ commemorate _____

5. blast, blow up, burst _____ erupt _____

6. fraud, faker, deceiver _____ hypocrite _____

7. warm, cook at a low heat _____ simmer _____

8. tiresome person; drill _____ bore _____

Part 2 Replace the underlined word(s) with a word from the box that means the same or almost the same. Write your answer on the line.

| gloat | duration | vast | wrangle |
| debut | oracle | irregular | |

9. After much rehearsal, the triumphant band had earned the right to brag.
_____ gloat _____

10. The introduction of the new cars will take place at the auto show.
_____ debut _____

11. The period of time of the junior high basketball game is usually 24 minutes.
_____ duration _____

12. The prophet foretold the future in riddles that no one could understand.
_____ oracle _____

13. Imagine how <u>enormous</u> the ocean must look to someone flying high in the sky.

_____ vast _____

14. Today, the seventh grade has an <u>odd</u> schedule of short class periods.

_____ irregular _____

15. The girls are starting to <u>brawl</u> again over who gets to ride the horse.

_____ wrangle _____

ANTONYMS

Antonyms are words that have opposite or nearly opposite meanings.

Part 1 Choose the word from the box that is the best antonym for each group of words. Write the word on the line.

| hypocrite | drought | commemorate | sturdy | vast |

1. flood, downpour, rainy season _____ drought _____

2. honest and sincere person _____ hypocrite _____

3. tiny, slight, small _____ vast _____

4. flimsy, feeble, weak _____ sturdy _____

5. discredit, dishonor _____ commemorate _____

Vocabulary in Action

Dust storms are sometimes caused by **drought** and land that has been overused. One of the worst droughts to hit the U.S. began in 1930. In Oklahoma, the drought led to terrible dust storms that were so powerful they destroyed crops and homes. The strong winds stirred up so much dirt that, at times, there was zero visibility and everything was covered in dirt. No matter how tightly Oklahomans sealed their homes, they could not keep the dirt from entering. By 1934, dust storms and drought had turned the Great Plains into a desert that came to be known as the Dust Bowl.

Part 2 Replace the underlined word(s) with a word from the box that means the opposite or almost the opposite. Write your answer on the line.

> acknowledge   simmer   wrangle   mental   irregular

6. The baseball took an unpredictable hop on the <u>smooth</u> playing field.

_____irregular_____

7. These long hikes are an unexpected <u>physical</u> challenge. _____mental_____

8. After you put in the noodles, allow the water to <u>boil furiously</u>.

_____simmer_____

9. James wondered if it was a good idea to <u>agree</u> with his wrestling coach.

_____wrangle_____

10. Do you <u>deny</u> that you used to like broccoli when you were little?

_____acknowledge_____

WORD STUDY

Prefixes Write the word from the box to complete each person's statement.

> overload   overflow   overcooked
>
> overpay   overcharge   oversleep

1. The butcher: I always carefully weigh each order, and I never

_____overcharge_____ my customers.

2. The chef: If by mistake we have _____overcooked_____ noodles, then we will make kugel, a baked pudding.

3. The engineer: We want to build the levy here so if the rivers

_____overflow_____, the water won't reach the homes.

4. The truck driver: It's a law. I never _____overload_____ the vehicle beyond its lawful capacity.

5. The shopper: I shop only for what I need; I check out the bargain table, and I never _____**overpay**_____ for anything.

6. The student: Even though I set my alarm clock, I still _____**oversleep**_____ and arrive late for school.

CHALLENGE WORDS

Word Learning—Challenge!

Study the spelling, part of speech, and meaning(s) of each word. Complete each sentence by writing the word on the line. Then read the sentence.

1. **elongate** *(v.)* to make longer or extend the length of

   You can _____**elongate**_____ a rubber band by pulling it.

2. **indispensable** *(adj.)* necessary or essential

   Presents are _____**indispensable**_____ parts of a birthday party.

3. **lubricate** *(v.)* 1. to make smooth; 2. to supply moisture

   Do we have more oil to _____**lubricate**_____ this machinery?

4. **pending** *(adj.)* not yet decided or determined

   The result of the _____**pending**_____ decision may affect our neighborhood.

5. **unscathed** *(adj.)* not harmed or injured

   Everyone else was hurt in the accident, but I was _____**unscathed**_____.

Use Your Vocabulary—Challenge!

I'm an Ant Imagine that you are an ant searching for food in a park where people are picnicking. On a separate sheet of paper, write a short story about your search for food, using the Challenge Words above. Be sure to describe how things smell, taste, and sound from your insect point of view.

FUN WITH WORDS

Read the first pair of words and think about the connection between them. Write the word from the box in each blank that creates a similar connection between the second pair of words.

reservoir	sturdy	irregular	bore
vast	hypocrite	digestion	drought
oracle	simmer		

1. heart is to circulation as stomach is to _____digestion_____

2. hot is to cold as flood is to _____drought_____

3. spokesperson is to company as _____oracle_____ is to a god

4. sand is to beach as water is to _____reservoir_____

5. smooth is to flat as uneven is to _____irregular_____

6. gentle is to rough as fragile is to _____sturdy_____

7. bake is to cake as _____simmer_____ is to soup

8. criminal is to crime as _____hypocrite_____ is to fraud

9. knit is to sweater as _____bore_____ is to hole

10. puddle is to small as ocean is to _____vast_____

Notable Quotes

"There were epochs in the history of humanity in which the writer was a sacred person. He wrote the sacred books, universal books, the codes, the epic, the **oracles.** Sentences inscribed on the walls of the crypts; examples in the portals of the temples. But in those times the writer was not an individual alone; he was the people."

—Augosto Roa Bastos (1913–2005), Paraguayan novelist

Review 10–12

Word Meanings Fill in the bubble of the word that is best defined by each phrase.

1. to admit something is true
   - a. bore
   - b. hustle
   - c. entrust
   - **d. acknowledge**

2. remarkable, fabulous, marvelous
   - a. irrational
   - **b. wondrous**
   - c. mental
   - d. oddly

3. to enliven and excite
   - **a. invigorate**
   - b. erupt
   - c. maul
   - d. gloat

4. to encourage in a friendly way
   - a. debut
   - b. bombard
   - **c. coax**
   - d. cringe

5. to combine efforts
   - a. simmer
   - b. stupefy
   - c. erupt
   - **d. collaborate**

6. troubled or distressed
   - a. strenuous
   - **b. distraught**
   - c. irregular
   - d. parallel

7. to accomplish a goal
   - a. wrangle
   - b. commemorate
   - c. duplicate
   - **d. prevail**

8. built in a solid way
   - a. ajar
   - **b. sturdy**
   - c. marine
   - d. shrill

9. showing longing
   - **a. wistful**
   - b. variable
   - c. dual
   - d. invalid

10. how long something lasts
    - **a. duration**
    - b. reservoir
    - c. epidemic
    - d. bough

11. a bodily disorder
    - a. alibi
    - b. drought
    - **c. ailment**
    - d. generator

12. the act of trusting
    - a. epidemic
    - **b. reliance**
    - c. criticism
    - d. ointment

13. a stopping or deterring
    - a. digestion
    - b. oracle
    - c. geologist
    - **d. prevention**

14. noisy in a happy, active way
    - a. irregular
    - b. ajar
    - **c. boisterous**
    - d. distraught

15. to communicate or express
    - **a. signify**
    - b. prevail
    - c. acknowledge
    - d. presume

16. huge in size
    - a. shrill
    - b. boisterous
    - c. wistful
    - **d. vast**

17. one who is a pretender
    - a. duration
    - **b. hypocrite**
    - c. relations
    - d. determination

18. to suppose or believe

    (a.) coax   **(b.)** wrangle   **(c.)** presume   **(d.)** hustle

19. to draw back in reaction to being scared or hurt

    (a.) cringe   **(b.)** invigorate   **(c.)** signify   **(d.)** gloat

20. a difference from what was planned or expected

    (a.) diameter   **(b.)** variation   **(c.)** alibi   **(d.)** ailment

Sentence Completion

Choose the word from the box that best completes each of the following sentences. Write the word in the blank.

bore	simmer	invalid	strenuous	debut
entrust	criticism	epidemic	duplicate	determination

1. I'd really like to attend the _____ **debut** _____ of the 10-year-old violinist on Friday night.

2. Doctors are working to prevent the spread of the disease so that it doesn't become a(n) _____ **epidemic** _____.

3. Many people have succeeded through hard work and _____ **determination** _____.

4. I find stamp collecting interesting, but my friends think it's a(n) _____ **bore** _____.

5. Most people respond better to praise than they do to _____ **criticism** _____.

6. How long should the sauce _____ **simmer** _____ before we add the vegetables?

7. Megan's argument was basically sound, but she did make a few _____ **invalid** _____ points.

8. Raking leaves is very _____ **strenuous** _____ work.

9. May I _____ **duplicate** _____ your famous cherry pie recipe?

10. Victoria knew better than to _____ **entrust** _____ her baseball card collection to her brother.

Fill in the Blanks
Choose the pair of words that best completes each sentence.

1. Emma _____ at the sound of the _____ crowd.
   - **a.** coaxed, dual
   - **b.** simmered, duplicate
   - **c.** presumed, wondrous
   - **d.** cringed, boisterous

2. Abigail was _____ about the _____ accusation.
   - **a.** distraught, irrational
   - **b.** sturdy, shrill
   - **c.** wistful, vast
   - **d.** stupefied, ajar

3. Believe it or not, _____ exercise can _____ you.
   - **a.** variable, coax
   - **b.** strenuous, invigorate
   - **c.** invalid, simmer
   - **d.** irregular, commemorate

4. Justin _____ he would be allowed to _____ with Alexander on the science project.
   - **a.** entrusted, stupefy
   - **b.** acknowledged, gloat
   - **c.** wrangled, prevail
   - **d.** presumed, collaborate

5. The _____ swore he had a(n) _____ for the time of the theft.
   - **a.** Marine, ointment
   - **b.** geologist, alibi
   - **c.** generator, epidemic
   - **d.** hypocrite, debut

6. There is practically no _____ between the original and the _____.
   - **a.** criticism, oracle
   - **b.** diameter, reservoir
   - **c.** determination, bore
   - **d.** variation, duplicate

7. The speaker refused to _____ the audience's _____.
   - **a.** commemorate, duration
   - **b.** hustle, variation
   - **c.** acknowledge, criticism
   - **d.** gloat, reliance

8. Keep your skis _____ if you want to avoid the _____ of sprawling in the snow.
   - **a.** parallel, humiliation
   - **b.** ajar, prevention
   - **c.** boisterous, digestion
   - **d.** duplicate, variation

9. School was closed for the _____ of the _____.
   - **a.** bough, reservoir
   - **b.** duration, epidemic
   - **c.** relations, ailment
   - **d.** criticism, variations

10. The _____ says she can see a(n) _____ image of future events.
    - **a.** hypocrite, wondrous
    - **b.** debut, irregular
    - **c.** bore, wistful
    - **d.** oracle, mental

Classifying Words

Sort the words in the box by writing each word to complete a phrase in the correct category.

acknowledge	ailment	criticism	debut	determination
diameter	droughts	erupt	geologist	gloat
invigorated	irrational	marine	ointment	prevention
reservoir	sturdy	variable	variations	vast

Words You Might Use to Talk About Health and Safety

1. the old saying that an ounce of _____prevention_____ is worth a pound of cure
2. climbing on a ladder that is strong and _____sturdy_____
3. seeing the doctor at the first sign of a(n) _____ailment_____
4. a brisk walk that makes you feel _____invigorated_____
5. an antiseptic _____ointment_____ in the first-aid kit

Words You Might Use to Talk About Acting

6. bowing to _____acknowledge_____ applause from the audience
7. making your _____debut_____ in a Broadway play
8. not letting thoughtless _____criticism_____ upset you
9. trying hard not to _____gloat_____ when you are called a star
10. holding on to your _____determination_____ when you don't get a part

Words You Might Use to Talk About Earth

11. the _____geologist_____ who learns the earth's history from rocks
12. volcanoes that _____erupt_____ without any warning
13. a formula for measuring the _____diameter_____ of the planet
14. trying to predict earthquakes, floods, and _____droughts_____
15. enjoying the _____variations_____ of the seasons

Words You Might Use to Talk About Water

16. the _____reservoir_____ that holds a city's supply of drinking water
17. snorkeling to come face-to-face with _____marine_____ creatures
18. trying to sail in _____variable_____ winds
19. a(n) _____irrational_____ fear of little minnows
20. standing on shore looking at the _____vast_____ ocean

CHAPTER 13

WORD LIST

Read each word using the pronunciation key.

altitude (al´ ti tōōd)
broker (brō´ kər)
commence (kə mens´)
compact (kom pakt´)
dedicate (ded´ ə kāt)
digestive (dī jes´ tiv)
eavesdrop (ēvz´ drop)
evolve (i vôlv´)
glorify (glôr´ ə fī)
hypodermic (hī pə dər´ mik)
irritable (ir´ ə tə bəl)
metallic (mə tal´ ik)
ovation (ō vā´ shən)
principle (prin´ sə pəl)
resign (ri zīn´)
schedule (skej´ ōōl)
simulate (sim´ yōō lāt)
submissive (səb mis´ iv)
veil (vāl)
writhe (rīth)

WORD STUDY

Analogies

Analogies show relationships between pairs of words. Study the relationships between the pairs of words in the analogies below.

bed is to **sleep** as **chair** is to **sit**

ring is to **finger** as **watch** is to **wrist**

den is to **fox** as **cave** is to **bat**

Challenge Words

interrogate (in târ´ ə gāt)
melancholy (mel´ ən käl ē)
pervade (pər vād´)
stalemate (stāl´ māt)
transcribe (tran skrīb´)

■ **TEACHER TIP: See page ix for suggestions on how to use this page.** *Level F*

WORDS IN CONTEXT

Read each sentence below to figure out the meaning of the word in **bold**. Use reasoning skills and the remainder of the sentence to help you. Write the meaning of the word on the line.

1. We hired a real estate **broker** to help us sell our house.

   <u>a person who is hired to buy or sell things for other people</u>

2. The hot-air balloon lifted us to an **altitude** of 1,200 feet above sea level.

   <u>the level or height above the surface of the earth</u>

3. At the end of the splendid concert, the band received a standing **ovation**.

   <u>an expression of approval or enjoyment by enthusiastic applause</u>

4. A **veil** of fog hid the football field from the spectators' view.

   <u>something that screens or hides</u>

5. I think tomato juice from a can has a **metallic** taste.

   <u>like metal</u>

6. How can you tell the leader of the pack from the more **submissive** wolves?

   <u>giving in to the power or control of another</u>

7. Sharon picked up the phone extension to **eavesdrop** on her sister's conversation.

   <u>to listen in secret to the conversations of others</u>

8. If I don't eat breakfast, I am a crabby and **irritable** person by midmorning.

   <u>easily made angry or impatient</u>

9. Bob **resigned** from his job so he could return to his college studies.

   <u>to give up a job</u>

10. The stomach and the small and large intestines are parts of the **digestive** system.

    <u>having to do with the process of digestion</u>

WORD MEANINGS

Word Learning

Study the spelling, part(s) of speech, and meaning(s) of each word. Complete each sentence by writing the word on the line. Then read the sentence.

1. **altitude** *(n.)* the level or height above the surface of the earth

   Our mountain hike took us to an _____ altitude _____ of 6,000 feet.

2. **broker** *(n.)* a person who is hired to buy or sell things for other people

   The antique _____ broker _____ offered $90 for our grandmother's gravy bowl.

3. **commence** *(v.)* 1. to start; 2. to begin

   We'll _____ commence _____ the pie-eating contest when I say, "Go!"

4. **compact** *(adj.)* packed tightly together; *(v.)* to pack or press tightly

   Roll your sleeping bag into a _____ compact _____ bundle.

   We can get all the luggage into the trunk if we _____ compact _____ it.

5. **dedicate** *(v.)* to commit or devote to something specific

   It's romantic to have someone _____ dedicate _____ a special song to you.

6. **digestive** *(adj.)* having to do with the process of digestion

   The next chapter in our health book will cover the _____ digestive _____ system.

7. **eavesdrop** *(v.)* to listen in secret to the conversations of others

   Sara hid in the closet in order to _____ eavesdrop _____ on the conversation.

8. **evolve** *(v.)* to develop or grow gradually

   Over time, the boys' rivalry will _____ evolve _____ into a strong friendship.

9. **glorify** *(v.)* 1. to give honor to; 2. to make distinguished; 3. to worship or praise

   New York had a big parade to _____ glorify _____ the returning astronauts.

10. **hypodermic** *(adj.)* injected or used to inject beneath the skin

    The nurse brought out a _____ hypodermic _____ needle, and Ty nearly fainted.

11. **irritable** *(adj.)* 1. easily made angry; 2. impatient; 3. oversensitive

    A tired and _____ irritable _____ baby needs to be put to bed for a nap.

12. **metallic** *(adj.)* 1. of or composed of metal; 2. like metal

The shimmer in the fabric was caused by its _____ metallic _____ threads.

13. **ovation** *(n.)* an expression of approval or enjoyment by enthusiastic applause

The Republicans sat quietly while the Democrats gave an _____ ovation _____.

14. **principle** *(n.)* a basic rule or standard

Honesty is a highly valued _____ principle _____ at the military academy.

15. **resign** *(v.)* 1. to give up a job; 2. to quit

Ill health has caused our librarian to _____ resign _____ from her position.

16. **schedule** *(n.)* a written list of events or appointments; *(v.)* to set the time for

The festival committee planned a busy _____ schedule _____ for the performers.

The judges will _____ schedule _____ one hour for each speaker.

17. **simulate** *(v.)* to imitate

Hang gliders _____ simulate _____ a bird's flight.

18. **submissive** *(adj.)* giving in to the power or control of another

Greta's mean dog becomes a _____ submissive _____ dog when she yells at him.

19. **veil** *(v.)* to cover or hide; *(n.)* something that screens or hides

The artist wants to _____ veil _____ the painting until the gallery opening.

The groom lifted the bride's _____ veil _____ and kissed her.

20. **writhe** *(v.)* 1. to squirm; 2. to twist

Snakes slither on the branches and _____ writhe _____ on the ground.

Notable Quotes

"Here's to the crazy ones, the misfits, the rebels, the troublemakers, the round pegs in the square holes . . . the ones who see things differently—they're not fond of rules. . . . You can quote them, disagree with them, **glorify** or vilify them, but the only thing you can't do is ignore them because they change things . . . they push the human race forward. And while some may see them as the crazy ones, we see genius, because the ones who are crazy enough to think that they can change the world are the ones who do."

—Steve Jobs (1955–), co-founder of Apple

Use Your Vocabulary

Choose the word from the Word List that best completes each sentence. Write the word on the line. You may use the plural form of nouns and the past tense of verbs if necessary.

Choosing a career to __1__ my life to is difficult. But it's time to __2__ my search for the perfect job. Of course, I have certain goals and __3__ that I would live my life by, such as having a career that allows me to serve others. With that in mind, I've thought about becoming a doctor, but I __4__ at the sight of __5__ needles. On the other hand, I could be a medical researcher and study a function of the body, such as the __6__ system. But hospitals make me uncomfortable.

I could be an airline pilot except I'm afraid of high __7__. I could be a(n) __8__, like my uncle who buys and sells stocks on Wall Street, but I can't even make my allowance last a whole week.

A friend of mine operates a machine that __9__ aluminum at a recycling center, but I don't like the __10__ sound of crunching cans. I've always thought it would be fun to be a travel agent and __11__ vacations for people, but I'd be disappointed and __12__ when I couldn't go too.

I could be a lion tamer in a circus and turn ferocious beasts into __13__ beasts, but I'm allergic to cats. Perhaps as an international spy, I could __14__ on important conversations. But I don't want to live my life under a(n) __15__ of secrecy, so maybe I should do something more out in the open.

I'd like to be an actor whom audiences __16__ and give standing __17__ to after each performance. Just one problem with that—I'm too shy to go onstage.

Maybe I will create computer programs that __18__ environmental and city problems, but I would have to learn about the problems first.

Oh well, I'm still young, so I suppose my talents will __19__ over time. And if I do pick a job that I don't like, I guess I always have an option to __20__ and try something else.

1. _____ dedicate
2. _____ commence
3. _____ principles
4. _____ writhe
5. _____ hypodermic
6. _____ digestive
7. _____ altitudes
8. _____ broker
9. _____ compacts
10. _____ metallic
11. _____ schedule
12. _____ irritable
13. _____ submissive
14. _____ eavesdrop
15. _____ veil
16. _____ glorify
17. _____ ovations
18. _____ simulate
19. _____ evolve
20. _____ resign

SYNONYMS

Synonyms are words that have the same or nearly the same meanings.

Part 1 Choose the word from the box that is the best synonym for each group of words. Write the word on the line.

evolve	irritable	commence	eavesdrop
glorify	principle	ovation	submissive

1. overhear, listen in, snoop   _____eavesdrop_____

2. unfold, expand, emerge   _____evolve_____

3. grumpy, ill-tempered, easily annoyed   _____irritable_____

4. applause, acclaim, cheers   _____ovation_____

5. passive, obedient, docile   _____submissive_____

6. originate, set forth, begin   _____commence_____

7. idolize, exalt, bless   _____glorify_____

8. rule, belief, law   _____principle_____

Part 2 Replace the underlined word(s) with a word from the box that means the same or almost the same. Write your answer on the line.

compact	veil	writhe	resign
simulate	schedule	altitude	

9. These candy worms <u>wiggle</u> just like real worms. _____writhe_____

10. Joey wants to go on the ride that claims to <u>mimic</u> a trip to the moon.
_____simulate_____

11. The airline pilot announced our cruising speed and <u>height</u> above sea level.
_____altitude_____

12. If you wish to see the doctor, you must have the secretary check his <u>calendar</u>.
_____schedule_____

13. Who could have guessed that Michael would <u>retire</u> from basketball to play baseball? _____resign_____

14. Some air fresheners only <u>mask</u> unpleasant odors, not eliminate them.
_____veil_____

15. If you <u>squeeze together</u> the aluminum cans, you can get more into the recycle box.
_____compact_____

ANTONYMS

Antonyms are words that have opposite or nearly opposite meanings.

Part 1 Choose the word from the box that is the best antonym for each group of words. Write the word on the line.

> writhe   resign   submissive   compact

1. take a job, keep working   _____resign_____

2. rest, be at ease, move easily   _____writhe_____

3. loose, slack; expand, draw apart   _____compact_____

4. active, resistant, willful   _____submissive_____

Part 2 Replace the underlined word with a word from the box that means the opposite or almost the opposite. Write your answer on the line.

> commence   irritable   glorify   veil

5. Grandmother remarked that Kyle had rather <u>pleasant</u> behavior at the dinner table.
_____irritable_____

6. This is the point where the rally will <u>end</u>. _____commence_____

7. The media is wrong to <u>condemn</u> the celebrity who has broken the law.
_____glorify_____

8. When the curtains open, the stage lighting will <u>reveal</u> the performers.
_____veil_____

Analogies To complete the following analogies, decide what kind of relationship is shown by the first pair of words. Then fill in the oval next to the pair of words that shows the same relationship.

1. **stove** is to **cook** as **car** is to _____
   - **a.** speed
   - **b.** ride
   - **c.** wash
   - **d.** bicycle

2. **enter** is to **door** as **climb** is to _____
   - **a.** tired
   - **b.** stairs
   - **c.** height
   - **d.** exit

3. **eavesdrop** is to **listen** as **argue** is to _____
   - **a.** mouth
   - **b.** anger
   - **c.** secret
   - **d.** speak

4. **audience** is to **ovation** as **actor** is to _____
   - **a.** people
   - **b.** theater
   - **c.** performance
   - **d.** costume

5. **veil** is to **cover** as **cry** is to _____
   - **a.** happy
   - **b.** weep
   - **c.** baby
   - **d.** soft

Vocabulary in Action

Interrogate is a transitive verb meaning "to question formally." It comes from the Latin *interrogatus*, the past participle of *interrogare*. It comes from the combination of *inter-* and *rogare*, meaning "to ask."

CHALLENGE WORDS

Word Learning—Challenge!

Study the spelling, part(s) of speech, and meaning(s) of each word. Complete each sentence by writing the word on the line. Then read the sentence.

1. **interrogate** *(v.)* to question formally

   Detectives will _____interrogate_____ the suspect about the crime.

2. **melancholy** *(n.)* a depressed state; *(adj.)* sad in spirit

   Happiness and _____melancholy_____ are opposite feelings.

   That _____melancholy_____ song makes me want to cry.

3. **pervade** *(v.)* to become spread out through every part of

   Rain will _____pervade_____ the entire state tonight.

4. **stalemate** *(n.)* 1. a standstill; 2. a contest that ends in a draw

   In a _____stalemate_____ between wrestlers, there is no winner or loser.

5. **transcribe** *(v.)* 1. to make a written copy; 2. to record

   A secretary will _____transcribe_____ the speech onto paper.

Use Your Vocabulary—Challenge!

A Day on the Job Imagine that in the future, you have become a police detective. On a separate sheet of paper, write a description of a typical day on the job, using the Challenge Words above. Be sure to describe your responsibilities and how you feel about your work.

> ## Vocabulary in Action
>
> In the mental health profession, *melancholia* is described as a depressive state. The **melancholy** person often experiences sadness, a lack of interest, and feelings of worthlessness. Through therapy, medication, or both of these treatments, the person may overcome the negative feelings and return to a healthier state.

FUN WITH WORDS

Your airplane has made an emergency landing on a faraway mountaintop. It will take three days for the rescue team to reach you. You have decided to record your thoughts and activities in a journal. You can write about one, two, or all three days of your adventure. However, to make writing in the journal more challenging, you must use at least eight of the vocabulary words from this chapter.

Answers will vary.

_____

_____

_____

_____

_____

_____

_____

_____

_____

_____

_____

_____

_____

_____

_____

Chapter 13   Level F

WORD LIST

Read each word using the pronunciation key.

ambiguous (am big´ yoō əs)
bulky (bul´ kē)
conceal (kən sēl´)
defect (dē´ fekt)
dignified (dig´ nə fīd)
elegance (el´ ə gəns´)
expedition (ek spə dish´ ən)
gnaw (nô)
identity (ī den´ ti tē)
integrate (in´ ti grāt)
meteoric (mēt ē ôr´ ik)
nautical (nôt´ i kəl)
negligent (neg´ li jənt)
nullify (nul´ ə fī)
pacifist (pas´ ə fist)
profit (prof´ it)
retaliate (ri tal´ ē āt)
scenic (sēn´ ik)
swindle (swin´ dəl)
velocity (və los´ ə tē)

WORD STUDY

Prefixes

The prefixes *il-*, *im-*, *in-*, and *ir-* are forms of the prefix *in-*, which means "not," "in," "into," or "within."

illegal (i lē´ gəl) *(adj.)* not legal
immeasurable (i mezh´ ər ə bəl) *(adj.)* too vast to be measured
immigrant (im´ ə grənt) *(n.)* a person who comes into a country to settle
incomplete (in kəm plēt´) *(adj.)* not complete
independent (in di pen´ dənt) *(adj.)* getting no help from others
irreversible (ir i vers´ ə bəl) *(adj.)* not able to be changed

Challenge Words

enchant (en chant´)
inflict (in flikt´)
lax (laks)
quaint (kwānt)
stifle (stī´ fəl)

■ **TEACHER TIP:** See page ix for suggestions on how to use this page.

Level F

WORDS IN CONTEXT

Read each sentence below to figure out the meaning of the word in **bold**. Use reasoning skills and the remainder of the sentence to help you. Write the meaning of the word on the line.

1. You must **conceal** Karen's birthday gift before she arrives so it will be a surprise.

   to hide or keep out of sight

2. It's too difficult for you to carry that **bulky** box by yourself.

   clumsy; large

3. The First Lady's gown for the inaugural ball gave her a look of **elegance**.

   distinction; good taste

4. My teacher will **integrate** the study of literature with the study of history.

   to blend into a whole

5. After six months, our restaurant made enough **profit** to allow us to expand.

   earnings from a business

6. My brother wears a white **nautical** uniform since he joined the U.S. Coast Guard.

   having to do with sailors, ships, or navigation

7. The tour bus driver thought we would enjoy the **scenic** drive to the beach.

   having an attractive or pleasing landscape

8. There is a stately and **dignified** painting of the senator hanging in the state capitol.

   noble; serious

9. An honest comic book salesperson would not **swindle** a collector.

   to cheat

10. During the storm, the wind **velocity** reached 80 miles per hour.

    rate of speed

WORD MEANINGS

Word Learning

Study the spelling, part(s) of speech, and meaning(s) of each word. Complete each sentence by writing the word on the line. Then read the sentence.

1. **ambiguous** *(adj.)* 1. unclear; 2. uncertain; 3. having more than one meaning

   "Maybe" is an _____**ambiguous**_____ answer to my request to go to the movies.

2. **bulky** *(adj.)* 1. clumsy; 2. massive; 3. large

   The movers stumbled up the stairs carrying the _____**bulky**_____ boxes.

3. **conceal** *(v.)* to hide or keep out of sight

   The jeweler will _____**conceal**_____ the jewels each night in a secret drawer.

4. **defect** *(n.)* 1. a flaw; 2. weakness; 3. imperfection

   The new stereo wouldn't work because of a _____**defect**_____ in the system.

5. **dignified** *(adj.)* 1. showing or expressing the quality of being worthy or honored; 2. having dignity; 3. noble; 4. serious

   The _____**dignified**_____ Southern gentleman escorted us to the opera.

6. **elegance** *(n.)* 1. good taste; 2. distinction

   The prince lived in a palace surrounded by _____**elegance**_____ and beauty.

7. **expedition** *(n.)* a journey undertaken for a specific purpose

   The purpose of the _____**expedition**_____ to the moon was to study rocks.

8. **gnaw** *(v.)* 1. to eat or chew at; 2. to erode or wear away

   A gerbil can _____**gnaw**_____ its way out of a cardboard box.

9. **identity** *(n.)* 1. individuality; uniqueness; 2. what or who a person or thing is

   A wolf in sheep's clothing is disguising its _____**identity**_____.

10. **integrate** *(v.)* 1. to bring together; 2. to blend into a whole

    The new plan will _____**integrate**_____ fifth grade into the middle school.

11. **meteoric** *(adj.)* 1. of or like a mass of stone or metal that comes toward Earth from outer space; 2. happening fast or suddenly

    After just one hit song, the singer had a _____**meteoric**_____ rise to stardom.

12. **nautical** *(adj.)* having to do with sailors, ships, or navigation

   Colorful _____nautical_____ flags fly from the boats.

13. **negligent** *(adj.)* indifferent; careless

   To improve his grades, Roy will need to improve his _____negligent_____ attitude.

14. **nullify** *(v.)* 1. to put an end to; 2. to make of no value; 3. to invalidate

   An outbreak of war will _____nullify_____ the peace treaty.

15. **pacifist** *(adj.)* of or relating to the opposition of war or violence; *(n.)* one who opposes war or violence

   The group Fathers Against Violence organized a _____pacifist_____ protest.

   Shanti went to India to live the life of a peace-loving _____pacifist_____.

16. **profit** *(n.)* 1. the earnings from a business; 2. a gain; 3. benefit; *(v.)* to create a gain from a business

   Our school store hopes to make a _____profit_____ on the sale of pencils.

   The Booster Club will _____profit_____ from a successful magazine sale.

17. **retaliate** *(v.)* to return or pay back a wrong, especially to get revenge

   Demetrius might _____retaliate_____ for your trick with a joke of his own.

18. **scenic** *(adj.)* having an attractive or a pleasing landscape

   The _____scenic_____ park along the Hudson River is a lovely picnic spot.

19. **swindle** *(v.)* 1. to cheat; 2. to trick; *(n.)* a fraud or cheating act

   The ticket scalper's aim was to _____swindle_____ the unsuspecting tourists.

   Unfortunately, the phony charity _____swindle_____ fooled many people.

20. **velocity** *(n.)* 1. quickness; 2. rate of speed

   The motorcycle sped past us with dangerous _____velocity_____.

Vocabulary in Action

A **pacifist** is a person who does not believe in using violence to achieve his or her goals. One of the most famous American pacifists is Jane Addams. Addams remained a peacemaker even when she was criticized for her views. Before World War I, Addams was probably the most beloved woman in America. A newspaper poll asked, "Who among our contemporaries are of the most value to the community?" Addams came in second, behind only Thomas Edison. She was strongly criticized, however, for opposing U.S. involvement in the war.

Use Your Vocabulary

Choose the word from the Word List that best completes each sentence. Write the word on the line. You may use the plural form of nouns and the past tense of verbs if necessary.

President Jefferson believed the United States would __1__ from greater knowledge of the West. He asked two explorers, Meriwether Lewis and William Clark, to lead a(n) __2__ from Missouri to Washington in the early 1800s. The explorers were instructed to undertake the journey as __3__. They were to promote peace with the Native Americans.

The men could not afford to be __4__ planners. Everything they would need had to be carried with them. __5__ items could not be taken on the journey. The __6__ of the Missouri River determined how far and how fast the boats could travel each day. Several men in the party had __7__ skills that proved useful on uncharted rivers.

Many of the men had __8__ feelings about meeting Native Americans for the first time. They had heard tales of Native Americans who tried to __9__ newcomers out of their horses. Some were afraid that the Native Americans would __10__ for problems caused by earlier explorers. Lewis and Clark asked a woman named Sacagawea to travel with them to explain their __11__ to the Native Americans. The explorers met a Mandan tribal leader who wore a headdress of great __12__. The man's leadership and __13__ manner were impressive.

Lewis and Clark wrote about the beautiful, __14__ surroundings, camping on the plains, and seeing __15__ rocks, often called shooting stars, falling across the sky. They were amazed by the prairie dogs that __16__ themselves in burrows. They were not pleased when the prairie dogs __17__ through bags of supplies.

Sometimes a boat would develop a(n) __18__, forcing them to stop and make repairs, or they would come upon the great waterfalls of the Missouri River. None of this could __19__ their eagerness to reach the Pacific Ocean and help __20__ the eastern and western parts of our country.

1. _____ profit
2. _____ expedition
3. _____ pacifists
4. _____ negligent
5. _____ Bulky
6. _____ velocity
7. _____ nautical
8. _____ ambiguous
9. _____ swindle
10. _____ retaliate
11. _____ identity
12. _____ elegance
13. _____ dignified
14. _____ scenic
15. _____ meteoric
16. _____ concealed
17. _____ gnawed
18. _____ defect
19. _____ nullify
20. _____ integrate

157

SYNONYMS

Synonyms are words that have the same or nearly the same meanings.

Part 1 Choose the word from the box that is the best synonym for each group of words. Write the word on the line.

velocity	conceal	defect	ambiguous
pacifist	bulky	retaliate	swindle

1. speed, quickness, swiftness   <u>velocity</u>

2. deceive; trick   <u>swindle</u>

3. failing, drawback   <u>defect</u>

4. vague, indefinite, obscure   <u>ambiguous</u>

5. big, awkward   <u>bulky</u>

6. screen, hide, cover   <u>conceal</u>

7. get revenge, repay, return   <u>retaliate</u>

8. peaceful; one who is antiwar   <u>pacifist</u>

Part 2 Replace the underlined word with a word from the box that means the same or almost the same. Write your answer on the line.

elegance	gnaw	integrate	expedition
negligent	profit	nullify	

9. The <u>proceeds</u> from the cookie sale will help pay for a trip to Mystic, Connecticut.
   <u>profit</u>

10. The salesperson showed us party dresses with grace and <u>style</u>.
    <u>elegance</u>

11. An Antarctic <u>voyage</u> is for the brave and hardy. <u>expedition</u>

12. A loss to their rival school will <u>stop</u> the team's chances for a championship.
    <u>nullify</u>

13. The rats are kept in wire cages so that they do not <u>bite</u> their way out.

<u>   gnaw   </u>

14. Ryan pays library fines because of his <u>neglectful</u> habit of returning books late.

<u> negligent </u>

15. I like the way our team of teachers <u>combines</u> language arts and writing.

<u> integrates </u>

 **ANTONYMS**

Antonyms are words that have opposite or nearly opposite meanings.

Part 1 Choose the word from the box that is the best antonym for each group of words. Write the word on the line.

> retaliate   nautical   negligent   scenic   defect

1. strength, perfection, virtue   <u> defect </u>

2. ignore, turn the other cheek   <u> retaliate </u>

3. careful, exact, mindful   <u> negligent </u>

4. having to do with land   <u> nautical </u>

5. not pleasing, unattractive   <u> scenic </u>

Part 2 Replace the underlined word with a word from the box that means the opposite or almost the opposite. Write your answer on the line.

> ambiguous   integrate   bulky   conceal   elegance

6. The students asked the principal to <u>separate</u> the boys' and girls' gym classes.

<u> integrate </u>

7. The truck driver washed her truck with amazing <u>roughness</u>.

<u> elegance </u>

8. A <u>small</u> load of laundry causes the washing machine to make a terrible noise.

<u> bulky </u>

9. The general expected to receive a <u>definite</u> answer from headquarters.

       <u>   ambiguous   </u>

10. Will the witness choose to <u>reveal</u> the true identity of the murderer?

       <u>   conceal   </u>

WORD STUDY

Prefixes Choose the word from the box that best completes each of the following sentences. Write the word in the blank.

illegal	immeasurable	immigrants
incomplete	independent	irreversible

1. Did you know that it's <u>   illegal   </u> to jaywalk across the street?

2. The damage was <u> irreversible </u>, so they tore down the building.

3. Allison's dishes don't match because she has an <u> incomplete </u> set.

4. Emma was grateful for everyone's <u> immeasurable </u> kindness.

5. My ancestors came to this country as <u> immigrants </u> from Ireland.

6. You'll be <u> independent </u> when you have an apartment of your own.

Vocabulary in Action

There are many synonyms for **quaint.** Some of them include *rustic, charming, old-fashioned, bucolic,* and *old-world.* *Quaint* is often used in books or novels to describe picturesque, rural settings.

CHALLENGE WORDS

Word Learning—Challenge!

Study the spelling, part(s) of speech, and meaning(s) of each word. Complete each sentence by writing the word on the line. Then read the sentence.

1. **enchant** *(v.)* to deeply attract or rouse to great admiration

   This song will _____ enchant _____ and fascinate you.

2. **inflict** *(v.)* 1. to give by striking; 2. to cause to be endured

   You must not _____ inflict _____ pain on other people.

3. **lax** *(adj.)* 1. not tense; loose; relaxed; 2. careless; 3. not strict enough

   A _____ lax _____ father should be more strict with his child.

4. **quaint** *(adj.)* unusual in an amusing or interesting way

   "Hickory, Dickory, Dock" is a _____ quaint _____ little rhyme.

5. **stifle** *(v.)* 1. to smother or suffocate; 2. to hold back

   Please _____ stifle _____ your sneezes with this handkerchief.

Use Your Vocabulary—Challenge!

A New Land Imagine that you are an explorer who has discovered a new land. On a separate sheet of paper, write a journal entry about your discovery. Use the Challenge Words above, and be sure to describe the people and the landscape.

> *Notable Quotes*
>
> "We shall match your capacity to **inflict** suffering with our capacity to endure it."
>
> —Martin Luther King, Jr. (1929–1968), civil-rights leader

FUN WITH WORDS

How carefully did you read the story on page 157? Write the vocabulary word that goes with each definition. Then unscramble the letters in the circles to form two words that tell what Lewis and Clark were trying to reach.

1. to hide
   Ⓒ O N Ⓒ E A L

2. to pay back a wrong
   R E T Ⓐ L Ⓘ A T E

3. of or like a stone that falls from space to earth
   M Ⓔ T E O R I Ⓒ

4. unclear
   Ⓐ M B I G U O U S

5. the earnings from a business
   Ⓟ R O F I T

6. to put an end to
   Ⓝ U L L I Ⓕ Y

7. to bring together
   Ⓘ N T E G R A T E

8. a journey for a specific purpose
   E X P E D I T I Ⓞ N

Answer: _____ PACIFIC OCEAN _____

WORD LIST

Read each word using the pronunciation key.

analyze (an´ ə līz)
bulletin (bŏol´ i tən)
confidential (kon fə den´ shəl)
delegate (n. del´ ə gət) (v. del´ ə gāt)
dignity (dig´ nə tē)
element (el´ ə mənt)
extraordinary (ek strôr´ də nâr ē)
gradual (gra´ jŏo wəl)
ignite (ig nīt´)
ingenious (in jēn´ yəs)
jovial (jō´ vē əl)
miniature (mi´ nē ə chŏor)
neutral (nŏo´ trəl)
parcel (pär´ səl)
puncture (puŋk´ chər)
retreat (ri trīt´)
slander (slan´ dər)
technical (tek´ ni kəl)
tendency (ten´ dən sē)
verge (vərj)

WORD STUDY

Root Words

The Latin root *capere* means "take." A root often changes its form, and *cap*, *cept*, and *ceipt* are forms of *capere*.

accept (ak sept´) (v.) to willingly take or receive
capacity (kə pas´ ə tē) (n.) the largest amount that can be held
capture (kap´ chər) (v.) to take by force
receipt (ri sēt´) (n.) a written statement that something has been received
receive (ri sēv´) (v.) to take into one's possession
reception (ri sep´ shən) (n.) a gathering to receive and welcome people

Challenge Words

lame (lām)
malady (mal´ ə dē)
malignant (mə lig´ nənt)
unique (yŏo nēk´)
vengeance (ven´ jəns)

■ **TEACHER TIP:** See page ix for suggestions on how to use this page.

Read each sentence below to figure out the meaning of the word in **bold**. Use reasoning skills and the remainder of the sentence to help you. Write the meaning of the word on the line.

1. The admiral's widow stood with **dignity** while the band played the Navy hymn.

   the condition of being worthy, honored, and respected

2. Lightning can **ignite** a tree and begin a forest fire.

   to set on fire

3. I have a **tendency** to talk a lot when I get nervous.

   a habit of acting or thinking a certain way

4. After several years of **gradual** growth, Jason shot up four inches over the summer.

   happening in small degrees or steps

5. Will you mail this **parcel** of newspaper clippings to Aunt Mary?

   a wrapped package

6. The class chose to send Carmen as our **delegate** to the convention.

   a representative

7. A nail will **puncture** a tire and cause it to flatten.

   to create a hole with something pointed or sharp

8. I always laugh in Mr. Chapa's class because he has a **jovial** personality.

   good-humored; full of fun

9. The Swiss took a **neutral** position during the war and stayed out of the conflict.

   not taking either side in a dispute

10. I haven't made up my mind yet, but I am on the **verge** of looking for a job.

    the point that something happens or begins

WORD MEANINGS

Word Learning

Study the spelling, part(s) of speech, and meaning(s) of each word. Complete each sentence by writing the word on the line. Then read the sentence.

1. **analyze** *(v.)* 1. to divide something into parts; 2. to examine thoroughly and in detail

   The doctor will first _____ **analyze** _____ the data, then make his diagnosis.

2. **bulletin** *(n.)* a brief statement of information or news

   The weather emergency _____ **bulletin** _____ flashed on the TV screen.

3. **confidential** *(adj.)* 1. relayed as a secret; 2. private

   The accountant keeps _____ **confidential** _____ reports in a locked cabinet.

4. **delegate** *(n.)* 1. a person with the authority to act for others; 2. a representative; *(v.)* to choose a person as a representative

   As our _____ **delegate** _____ to the convention, Mrs. Cohn will cast our vote.

   The teacher will _____ **delegate** _____ students to do the classroom tasks.

5. **dignity** *(n.)* the condition of being worthy, honored, and respected

   The Egyptian president's funeral was conducted with great _____ **dignity** _____.

6. **element** *(n.)* 1. one of more than one hundred basic substances from which all things are made; 2. a simple part

   Gold is an _____ **element** _____ with great value.

7. **extraordinary** *(adj.)* 1. unusual; 2. remarkable; 3. uncommon

   Thomas Jefferson had an _____ **extraordinary** _____, inventive mind.

8. **gradual** *(adj.)* 1. happening in small degrees or steps; 2. little by little

   Regular, _____ **gradual** _____ savings is better than not saving money at all.

9. **ignite** *(v.)* 1. to set on fire; 2. to begin to burn

   _____ **Ignite** _____ the kindling first when you build a fire in the fireplace.

10. **ingenious** *(adj.)* 1. inventive; 2. clever

    Earl amazed his boss with his _____ **ingenious** _____ time-saving invention.

11. **jovial** *(adj.)* 1. good-humored; 2. full of fun; 3. merry

    Our family reunions are great fun due to our _____ **jovial** _____ Uncle Frank.

12. **miniature** *(adj.)* created or made on a very tiny scale

    Even today, a _____ miniature _____ Statue of Liberty is a prized souvenir.

13. **neutral** *(adj.)* 1. not taking either side in a dispute; 2. uninvolved

    The _____ neutral _____ countries will not support either warring nation.

14. **parcel** *(n.)* a wrapped package

    I need string and paper to wrap the _____ parcel _____ before mailing it.

15. **puncture** *(n.)* a hole that is created by something pointed or sharp; *(v.)* to create a hole with something pointed or sharp

    Joe got the _____ puncture _____ patched and put the tire back on the car.

    The object of the game was to _____ puncture _____ the balloon with a dart.

16. **retreat** *(v.)* 1. to go or move back; 2. to withdraw from something; *(n.)* the act of moving back or withdrawing

    To save themselves, the residents will _____ retreat _____ from the high water.

    The beekeeper made a hasty _____ retreat _____ from the overturned beehive.

17. **slander** *(v.)* to talk falsely or incorrectly about someone; *(n.)* a false or an incorrect statement meant to harm another person's reputation

    Newspapers behave irresponsibly when they _____ slander _____ celebrities.

    The radio broadcasts spread _____ slander _____ about the enemy.

18. **technical** *(adj.)* having to do with a mechanical or scientific subject

    Cara, a _____ technical _____ writer, edits computer manuals.

19. **tendency** *(n.)* a habit of acting or thinking a certain way

    Mom has a _____ tendency _____ to worry about me, but I'm glad she does.

20. **verge** *(n.)* 1. the point that something happens or begins; 2. the brink

    The year 2000 was the _____ verge _____ of a new century and a new millennium.

Vocabulary in Action

In 1853, José Manuel Gallegos became the second Hispanic U.S. representative in history. Gallegos left Washington after his second term. He returned to the House of Representatives in 1873, however, once again as a **delegate** from the territory of New Mexico.

Use Your Vocabulary

Choose the word from the Word List that best completes each sentence. Write the word on the line. You may use the plural form of nouns and the past tense of verbs if necessary.

The personal computer is one of the most important **1** advances of the century. Its **2** design makes computers user-friendly. This is the chief reason for the personal computer's **3** popularity. One important **4** of the computer's inner workings is the microchip. Because the **5** microchip is small in size but big in capability, it helped **6** a computer revolution that spread like wildfire.

My teacher, a very **7** person, wants my class to have fun as we apply our computer knowledge to something interesting. So we are using a computer to **8** the cost and effectiveness of a variety of headache medicines. We're also investigating the advertising of competitive medications to determine whether the ads are **9** or truth. We are trying to take a(n) **10** position in our analysis and not recommend one medication over another. As a result of this study, I have been asked to be a(n) **11** to the computer fair, where I will present our results and represent our school with honor and **12** .

When I'm at home, I sometimes **13** to my room to play games on my computer. I can keep all my game scores private by assigning a(n) **14** password to the computer program. But my parents say I have a(n) **15** to spend too much time on the computer and not enough time on my homework. They are not trying to **16** my dreams of being a computer wizard, but are concerned that I might neglect other subjects.

Until last week, I was on the **17** of buying a more powerful computer with the money I've been saving. I had been reading **18** on the Internet to keep track of the new computers and their prices. Then a surprise **19** came in the mail. It was my uncle's old computer, which is much more powerful than mine. I've been taking a(n) **20** approach to learning all it can do.

1. _____ technical _____
2. _____ ingenious _____
3. _____ extraordinary _____
4. _____ element _____
5. _____ miniature _____
6. _____ ignite _____
7. _____ jovial _____
8. _____ analyze _____
9. _____ slander _____
10. _____ neutral _____
11. _____ delegate _____
12. _____ dignity _____
13. _____ retreat _____
14. _____ confidential _____
15. _____ tendency _____
16. _____ puncture _____
17. _____ verge _____
18. _____ bulletins _____
19. _____ parcel _____
20. _____ gradual _____

SYNONYMS

Synonyms are words that have the same or nearly the same meanings.

Part 1 Choose the word from the box that is the best synonym for each group of words. Write the word on the line.

retreat	tendency	parcel	ignite
verge	neutral	ingenious	miniature

1. edge, limit, boundary _____ verge _____

2. leaning, bent, likelihood _____ tendency _____

3. fall back, move away from _____ retreat _____

4. bundle, packet, package _____ parcel _____

5. standing by, inactive, unconcerned _____ neutral _____

6. little, small, tiny _____ miniature _____

7. light, burst into flames, burn _____ ignite _____

8. bright, keen, intelligent _____ ingenious _____

Part 2 Replace the underlined word with a word from the box that means the same or almost the same. Write your answer on the line.

jovial	analyze	confidential	extraordinary
gradual	bulletin	dignity	

9. A friendly, <u>jolly</u> greeter welcomes shoppers at the store's entrance.
_____ jovial _____

10. The trucks on the highway made only <u>slow</u> progress in the blizzard.
_____ gradual _____

11. The police will carefully <u>study</u> the hostage situation before taking action.
_____ analyze _____

12. The public-address system crackled, and then we heard the morning announcement. _____ bulletin _____

13. Liz keeps her diary locked because it is <u>personal</u>. _____confidential_____

14. The conductor directed the band to play "Hail to the Chief" with <u>honor</u>. _____dignity_____

15. Niagara Falls is an <u>incredible</u> sight. _____extraordinary_____

ANTONYMS

Antonyms are words that have opposite or nearly opposite meanings.

Part 1 Choose the word from the box that is the best antonym for each group of words. Write the word on the line.

> extraordinary   neutral   gradual   confidential   ignite

1. known to all, public _____confidential_____

2. involved, taking an active part _____neutral_____

3. sudden, hasty, all at once _____gradual_____

4. usual, normal, ordinary _____extraordinary_____

5. extinguish, put out, quench _____ignite_____

Part 2 Replace the underlined word(s) with a word from the box that means the opposite or almost the opposite. Write your answer on the line.

> slander   miniature   ingenious   jovial   retreat

6. Bunk beds in my room are an <u>inept</u> solution to make more space. _____ingenious_____

7. With Aunt Sarah visiting, we have many <u>cheerless</u> dinners. _____jovial_____

8. We have <u>full-sized</u> horses in the barn. _____miniature_____

9. Readers should know that the unauthorized biography is full of <u>truth</u>. _____slander_____

10. At the height of battle, General Lee ordered his troops to <u>advance</u>. _____retreat_____

Root Words The word meanings in the circles come from the Latin root *capere*. The word meanings are different, but all are related to the meaning "take." Complete the word web with these *capere* words.

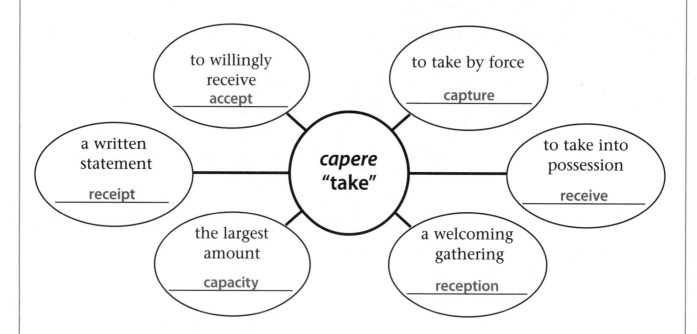

to willingly receive
____accept____

to take by force
____capture____

a written statement
____receipt____

capere "take"

to take into possession
____receive____

the largest amount
____capacity____

a welcoming gathering
____reception____

CHALLENGE WORDS

Word Learning—Challenge!

Study the spelling, part(s) of speech, and meaning(s) of each word. Complete each sentence by writing the word on the line. Then read the sentence.

1. **lame** *(adj.)* physically disabled or weak

   The _____**lame**_____ horse had trouble walking.

2. **malady** *(n.)* a disease or disorder

   What _____**malady**_____ made you so sick?

3. **malignant** *(adj.)* tending to produce death, destruction, or deterioration

   _____**Malignant**_____ wounds were a cause of death in the Civil War.

4. **unique** *(adj.)* 1. being the only one; 2. unusual

   This _____**unique**_____, one-of-a-kind watch is not for sale.

5. **vengeance** *(n.)* punishment in retaliation for an offense

   I seek _____**vengeance**_____ for the wrongs you have done to me.

Use Your Vocabulary—Challenge!

The Cure You have created a medicine to cure a disease. Write directions on how to make this medicine, using the Challenge Words above. Be sure to describe the ingredients and how you put them together.

> ### Notable Quotes
>
> "In the right light, at the right time, everything is **extraordinary**."
>
> —Aaron Rose (1940–), writer, director, founder of Beautiful Losers art movement

FUN WITH WORDS

Unscramble the vocabulary words. Then write the letter of the definition that matches each unscrambled word.

1. greev   _verge_   _g_   **a.** a package

2. teagleed   _delegate_   _n_   **b.** uninvolved

3. drensal   _slander_   _k_   **c.** private information

4. tieing   _ignite_   _i_   **d.** to make a hole

5. cendenyt   _tendency_   _o_   **e.** inventive

6. laudarg   _gradual_   _l_   **f.** unusual

7. eniousing   _ingenious_   _e_   **g.** the beginning point

8. denfinoctial   _confidential_   _c_   **h.** about a scientific subject

9. menteel   _element_   _m_   **i.** to set on fire

10. lautner   _neutral_   _b_   **j.** a brief statement of news

11. tublenil   _bulletin_   _j_   **k.** to talk falsely about

12. draniroartexy   _extraordinary_   _f_   **l.** happening little by little

13. chentacil   _technical_   _h_   **m.** a simple part

14. renupcut   _puncture_   _d_   **n.** a representative

15. crelap   _parcel_   _a_   **o.** a habit

Review 13–15

Word Meanings Underline the word that is best defined by each phrase.

1. loud and long applause
   a. elegance   **b. ovation**   c. dignity   d. puncture

2. height above the ground
   a. altitude   b. identity   c. ovation   d. expedition

3. speed of something
   a. delegate   b. element   c. broker   **d. velocity**

4. not careful
   a. nautical   b. scenic   **c. negligent**   d. compact

5. to go backward
   a. retreat   b. eavesdrop   c. gnaw   d. altitude

6. a basic law
   a. pacifist   b. puncture   **c. principle**   d. profit

7. to put out of sight
   a. conceal   b. ignite   c. dedicate   d. retaliate

8. fun-loving and jolly
   a. submissive   **b. jovial**   c. meteoric   d. extraordinary

9. very small
   a. ambiguous   **b. miniature**   c. submissive   d. dignified

10. to quit or retire
    a. schedule   b. simulate   c. swindle   **d. resign**

11. an imperfect part
    a. defect   b. velocity   c. slander   d. principle

12. so big as to be awkward
    a. bulky   b. hypodermic   c. confidential   d. ingenious

13. to begin
    a. evolve   **b. commence**   c. glorify   d. integrate

14. joining neither side in a war
    a. irritable   b. gradual   c. technical   **d. neutral**

15. to study the parts of something
    a. writhe   b. nullify   **c. analyze**   d. slander

16. a necessary or basic part
    (a.) broker   (**b.**) element   (c.) veil   (d.) verge

17. noble and proper
    (a.) jovial   (b.) digestive   (c.) nautical   (**d.**) dignified

18. to do harm in return for harm done
    (a.) evolve   (**b.**) retaliate   (c.) resign   (d.) eavesdrop

19. something that covers or hides
    (a.) parcel   (b.) bulletin   (c.) profit   (**d.**) veil

20. relating to science
    (a.) meteoric   (b.) metallic   (**c.**) technical   (d.) hypodermic

Sentence Completion Choose the word from the box that best completes each of the following sentences. Write the word in the blank.

integrated	tendency	expedition	digestive	simulate
bulletin	extraordinary	scheduled	identity	gnawed

1. In the stomach, _____ digestive _____ juices break down food.

2. The squirrel _____ gnawed _____ a hole in the telephone wire.

3. My cousin was asked to demonstrate her _____ extraordinary _____ juggling skills.

4. Ana and Thomas are planning a(n) _____ expedition _____ to South America.

5. The latest weather _____ bulletin _____ said a thunderstorm is approaching.

6. In drama class, we were asked to _____ simulate _____ an elephant walking.

7. Peter did not reveal his _____ identity _____ until the end of the costume party.

8. Have you _____ scheduled _____ a meeting with the principal?

9. I have a(n) _____ tendency _____ to ignore my alarm clock in the morning.

10. The band director _____ integrated _____ the sounds of all the instruments into a pleasing melody.

Fill in the Blanks Underline the pair of words that best completes each sentence.

1. A person who would _____ may be a person without high _____.
   - **a.** eavesdrop, principles
   - **b.** conceal, bulletins
   - **c.** swindle, ovations
   - **d.** resign, parcels

2. The convention _____ attended a _____ meeting.
   - **a.** expedition, gradual
   - **b.** pacifists, miniature
   - **c.** delegates, confidential
   - **d.** brokers, metallic

3. The company president is _____ and friendly, but she has _____ too.
   - **a.** jovial, dignity
   - **b.** neutral, velocity
   - **c.** irritable, elegance
   - **d.** negligent, schedules

4. The scientists _____ the meteor fragments and reported that they were _____.
   - **a.** integrated, submissive
   - **b.** ignited, technical
   - **c.** concealed, irritable
   - **d.** analyzed, metallic

5. According to the _____, the game will _____ at exactly 7:05.
   - **a.** slander, swindle
   - **b.** schedule, commence
   - **c.** altitude, nullify
   - **d.** velocity, retaliate

6. The amusement park ride _____ a(n) _____ to the North Pole.
   - **a.** punctures, broker
   - **b.** identifies, tendency
   - **c.** simulates, expedition
   - **d.** evolves, veil

7. The package is _____ but it contains a(n) _____ surprise.
   - **a.** bulky, extraordinary
   - **b.** compact, submissive
   - **c.** scenic, nautical
   - **d.** ambiguous, neutral

8. The author _____ his book to his _____ schnauzer.
   - **a.** nullified, negligent
   - **b.** gnawed, jovial
   - **c.** integrated, confidential
   - **d.** dedicated, miniature

9. The _____ hopes his new business will begin to show a(n) _____ quickly.
   - **a.** bulletin, defect
   - **b.** delegate, element
   - **c.** puncture, dignity
   - **d.** broker, profit

10. The mountain climbers were on the _____ of reaching the peak when a snowstorm forced them to _____.
    - **a.** verge, retreat
    - **b.** altitude, swindle
    - **c.** velocity, profit
    - **d.** elegance, defect

Classifying Words
Sort the words in the box by writing each word to complete a phrase in the correct category.

altitude	bulletin	commence	concealed	dedicates
defects	expedition	extraordinary	identity	jovial
meteoric	negligent	ovation	pacifist	parcels
schedule	submissive	swindled	technical	velocity

Words You Might Use to Talk About Personalities

1. a main character that is careless and _____negligent_____

2. a professor who _____dedicates_____ her life to her job

3. a former soldier who is now a(n) _____pacifist_____

4. a grandfather who is always kind and _____jovial_____

5. a well-trained dog that is _____submissive_____ to her owner

Words You Might Use to Talk About Airplane Trips

6. checking the _____schedule_____ to see if your flight is on time

7. flying at a(n) _____altitude_____ of 35,000 feet

8. the copilot's _____technical_____ knowledge

9. flight attendants stowing _____parcels_____ in the overhead bins

10. no _____defects_____ in the landing gear

Words You Might Use to Talk About the Weather

11. a special _____bulletin_____ about the hurricane

12. a(n) _____meteoric_____ rise in temperature in just one hour

13. a(n) _____extraordinary_____ winter warm spell

14. a late snowfall that _____concealed_____ blooming plants

15. high- _____velocity_____ winds that knocked down power lines

Words You Might Use to Talk About the News

16. a stock broker who _____swindled_____ innocent customers

17. a new space program that is about to _____commence_____

18. a music star who gets a standing _____ovation_____ at her concert

19. the unknown _____identity_____ of the suspect

20. the latest report about the _____expedition_____ to Antarctica

Posttest

Choosing the Definitions Fill in the bubble of the item that best defines the word in bold in each sentence.

Ch. 7 **1.** Katelyn's smile is as welcoming as a **beacon** in the night.
  a. snack   **(b.)** light   **c.** yell   **d.** dream

Ch. 3 **2.** From an early age, Michelle knew her **vocation** was to be a doctor.
  a. schedule   **b.** free time   **(c.)** career   **d.** specialty

Ch. 5 **3.** Since they bought their trailer, Grandma and Grandpa are **nomads** every winter.
  (a.) wanderers   **b.** elderly   **c.** campers   **d.** homeless

Ch. 12 **4.** The speaker chose not to **acknowledge** the other candidate's presence.
  a. ignore   **b.** sense   **c.** give back   **(d.)** recognize

Ch. 14 **5.** Vanessa loves to snuggle inside her **bulky** overcoat on snowy winter days.
  a. colorful   **(b.)** large   **c.** warm   **d.** old

Ch. 4 **6.** The process for solving the math problem was **incomprehensible** to Evan.
  a. easy   **b.** understandable   **(c.)** unclear   **d.** known

Ch. 14 **7.** The members of the party have a **pacifist** agenda.
  a. childish   **b.** rowdy   **c.** effective   **(d.)** antiwar

Ch. 15 **8.** No matter how hard she tried, Erin could not **puncture** the balloon.
  (a.) pop   **b.** hang   **c.** blow up   **d.** fill

Ch. 11 **9.** The trees lost several **boughs** in the storm.
  a. leaves   **b.** pinecones   **(c.)** branches   **d.** trunks

Ch. 2 **10.** Alex was willing to **grovel** before the judge to get his fine reduced.
  a. speak softly   **(b.)** humble oneself   **c.** walk proudly   **d.** quiver

Ch. 13 **11.** The plane was flying at a dangerous **altitude**.
  a. angle   **b.** speed   **(c.)** height   **d.** temperature

Ch. 12 **12.** Because of the **drought**, the corn crop was sparse.
  a. flood   **b.** fire   **c.** insects   **(d.)** dry period

Ch. 10 **13.** The ingenious invention has a **dual** purpose.
  (a.) double   **b.** boring   **c.** noble   **d.** unusual

Ch. 8 **14.** The neighbors joined together to clean up the **urban** playground.
  a. dirty   **b.** rural   **c.** school   **(d.)** city

Ch. 2 **15.** The architect planned an **annex** for the old school building.
  a. playground   **(b.)** expansion   **c.** shed   **d.** landscape

177

Ch. 14 16. The president wrote a **dignified** response to the child's letter.
    a. angry   **b.** slow   **c.** bold   **d.** serious

Ch. 7 17. I saw the rescue workers **weaving** through the crowd.
    a. jogging   **b.** twisting   **c.** crying   **d.** skipping

Ch. 6 18. The flood waters **engulfed** the small island.
    a. floated   **b.** enclosed   **c.** submerged   **d.** moistened

Ch. 9 19. We gasped as we watched the **aerial** stunt.
    a. risky   **b.** on the ground   **c.** in the air   **d.** successful

Ch. 14 20. The builders didn't see the **defect** in the plan until they tried to carry it out.
    a. weakness   **b.** surprise   **c.** detail   **d.** change

Ch. 9 21. The city council will **debate** the new law at tonight's meeting.
    a. pass   **b.** overturn   **c.** write   **d.** discuss

Ch. 7 22. I wonder how Carlos will **react** to the bad news.
    a. ignore   **b.** hurry   **c.** respond   **d.** deny

Ch. 10 23. The diplomats struggled to build good **relations** between the two nations.
    a. connections   **b.** health   **c.** records   **d.** moods

Ch. 11 24. The boys thought it was fun to **collaborate** on the song.
    a. learn to play   **b.** make fun of   **c.** listen to   **d.** work together

Ch. 9 25. Everyone worked hard to make the **division** of the bake sale money fair.
    a. spending   **b.** sharing   **c.** saving   **d.** counting

Ch. 10 26. The nurse says Andrea will recover from the **ailment** quickly.
    a. shock   **b.** illness   **c.** journey   **d.** operation

Ch. 4 27. Elijah was proud when the dentist said he didn't have even one **cavity**.
    a. crooked tooth   **b.** filling   **c.** hole in a tooth   **d.** tantrum

Ch. 14 28. The leaders hoped to be able to **integrate** the groups from the two different schools smoothly.
    a. compare   **b.** study   **c.** talk to   **d.** combine

Ch. 13 29. My new baby brother is cute when he is not being **irritable**.
    a. grumpy   **b.** calm   **c.** sweet   **d.** sleeping

Ch. 15 30. Isabella was carrying so many **parcels** she was afraid she would drop one.
    a. umbrellas   **b.** packages   **c.** kittens   **d.** books

Word Relations

Synonyms are words that have the same or nearly the same meanings. Antonyms are words that have opposite or nearly opposite meanings. In the blank before each pair of words, write *S* if the words are synonyms, *A* if they are antonyms, or *N* if they are not related.

1. __N__ nullify   associate

2. __A__ reveal   veil

3. __A__ glorify   slander

4. __N__ hypodermic   absorb

5. __S__ stir   invigorate

6. __A__ ignite   quench

7. __S__ duplicate   simulate

8. __N__ civilize   signify

9. __S__ acute   keen

10. __A__ serene   frantic

11. __N__ oracle   ointment

12. __S__ whisk   hustle

13. __A__ manipulate   coax

14. __N__ inevitable   dissolve

15. __S__ besiege   bombard

16. __N__ illicit   enlist

17. __N__ digestion   prevention

18. __A__ compact   vast

19. __S__ deter   impede

20. __A__ retaliate   negotiate

21. __S__ ingenious   extraordinary

22. __A__ literal   figurative

23. __N__ slogan   debate

24. __A__ mental   physical

25. __S__ fierce   savage

26. __N__ trifle   tedious

27. __S__ ambiguous   incomprehensible

28. __A__ discontent   contentment

29. __N__ scholar   scoundrel

30. __S__ nobility   dignity

Using Context Clues

Fill in the bubble of the phrase that best completes each sentence.

Ch. 3 1. If you travel to an **exotic** land, you will go
- (a.) across the river.
- (b.) over a mountain.
- (c.) to your neighbor's house.
- (d.) to a foreign country.

Ch. 12 2. Richard felt like a **hypocrite** when he
- (a.) missed the last bus.
- (b.) said his name was Tristan.
- (c.) sang out of tune.
- (d.) rescued the stranded kitten.

Ch. 14 3. When she saw the restaurant's **elegance**, Jenna exclaimed,
- (a.) "Can we go somewhere else?"
- (b.) "I'd like some dessert."
- (c.) "What good taste the owners have!"
- (d.) "What an ugly place!"

Ch. 1 **4.** An **angle** can always be found in
- (a.) a teardrop.
- (b.) an automobile tire.
- (c.) a globe.
- (d.) a baseball diamond.

Ch. 13 **5.** If your **digestive** system isn't working properly, you
- (a.) may have a stomachache.
- (b.) may have trouble breathing.
- (c.) should get help from a gardener.
- (d.) should get help from a banker.

Ch. 10 **6.** Shelby avoided **strenuous** activity after
- (a.) the stove broke.
- (b.) she hurt her back.
- (c.) her parents returned.
- (d.) she learned to swim.

Ch. 12 **7.** If a crowd **erupts** after a concert, it
- (a.) leaves quietly.
- (b.) goes backstage.
- (c.) cheers and claps loudly.
- (d.) sits back down.

Ch. 3 **8.** When Nathaniel saw Chloe **sneer**, he knew she
- (a.) wanted to eat lunch.
- (b.) was very excited.
- (c.) wanted to talk to him.
- (d.) was still mad at him.

Ch. 6 **9.** A **spectrum** in the sky is
- (a.) a rainbow.
- (b.) an airplane.
- (c.) a shooting star.
- (d.) a full moon.

Ch. 13 **10.** After Melissa **resigned** as president of the Spanish Club,
- (a.) she mailed the letter.
- (b.) she changed the club's rules.
- (c.) the club elected a new president.
- (d.) the club welcomed her with a party.

Ch. 8 **11.** We spent all afternoon digging a **shaft** for
- (a.) a doghouse.
- (b.) a new well.
- (c.) a treehouse.
- (d.) a driveway.

Ch. 1 **12.** If you feel the ground **vibrate**, you may be
- (a.) under a bridge.
- (b.) running too fast.
- (c.) in a hurricane.
- (d.) in an earthquake.

Ch. 8 **13.** If someone speaks with **clarity**,
- (a.) it is difficult to respond.
- (b.) she is in a hurry.
- (c.) she is easy to understand.
- (d.) you can't hear the words.

Ch. 15 **14.** To **analyze** the test results, you must
- (a.) study them closely.
- (b.) take the test yourself.
- (c.) tell everyone about them.
- (d.) tell no one about them.

Ch. 15 **15.** The king lost his **dignity** for a moment when he
  (a.) forgot where he put it.
  (b.) dropped it in the river.
  (c.) woke up this morning.
  (d.) tripped on his robe.

Ch. 10 **16.** When you **presume** that you're invited to a party, you
  (a.) know for a fact you are invited.
  (b.) assume that you are invited.
  (c.) are upset that you are not invited.
  (d.) aren't sure you are invited.

Ch. 2 **17.** You may sign up for the "**Juvenile** Jog" if you are
  (a.) an athlete.
  (b.) a grandparent.
  (c.) under 15 years old.
  (d.) over 25 years old.

Ch. 6 **18.** If you have an **obligation** to babysit, you
  (a.) have promised to babysit.
  (b.) do not enjoy babysitting.
  (c.) are paid to watch small children.
  (d.) babysit for free.

Ch. 1 **19.** The doctor looked at Kiara's **pupils** after he gave her
  (a.) braces.
  (b.) bandages.
  (c.) fillings.
  (d.) eye drops.

Ch. 11 **20.** One of Patrick's answers was **invalid**, but the others were
  (a.) wrong.
  (b.) sad.
  (c.) correct.
  (d.) not logical.

Ch. 3 **21.** An animal in **captivity** would probably
  (a.) fly away.
  (b.) live in the wild.
  (c.) live in a cage.
  (d.) control its own life.

Ch. 1 **22.** Something made of **granite** would
  (a.) feel very hard.
  (b.) be soft as a pillow.
  (c.) bend in the wind.
  (d.) be light as a feather.

Ch. 5 **23.** A person who is **gullible**
  (a.) keeps birds for a hobby.
  (b.) is always in a bad mood.
  (c.) believes whatever you say.
  (d.) is very suspicious.

Ch. 8 **24.** If you take the **initiative**, you
  (a.) are afraid to go first.
  (b.) may become known as a leader.
  (c.) may serve time in prison.
  (d.) are willing to wait a while.

Ch. 10 **25.** A **boisterous** crowd
  (a.) is quiet and sad.
  (b.) includes only men.
  (c.) is marching in rows.
  (d.) is loud and rowdy.

Analogies
Analogies show relationships between pairs of words.

To complete the analogies, decide what kind of relationship is shown by the first pair of words. Then fill in the bubble of the other pair of words that show the same relationship.

Ch. 6 1. bankrupt is to **wealthy** as
- a. active is to busy
- b. sunny is to clear
- c. healthy is to ill
- d. mischievous is to naughty

Ch. 9 2. obstacle is to **deter** as
- a. shovel is to rake
- b. gate is to fence
- c. leisure is to work
- d. trap is to entangle

Ch. 15 3. jovial is to **celebration** as
- a. duty is to voluntary
- b. ingenious is to smart
- c. destructive is to blight
- d. valiant is to coward

Ch. 2 4. perch is to **bird** as
- a. oven is to heat
- b. crouch is to lion
- c. beat is to rhythm
- d. pigment is to skin

Ch. 4 5. radiant is to **dim** as
- a. timid is to shy
- b. inept is to clumsy
- c. annoying is to bothersome
- d. fresh is to stale

Ch. 6 6. gully is to **hill** as
- a. ocean is to desert
- b. valley is to ditch
- c. velocity is to speed
- d. ambiguous is to question

Ch. 6 7. destructive is to **hurtful** as
- a. physical is to musical
- b. polite is to rude
- c. shiny is to dull
- d. appreciative is to thankful

Ch. 9 8. generate is to **produce** as
- a. debate is to agree
- b. migrate is to settle
- c. accelerate is to speed up
- d. despise is to love

Ch. 1 9. abominable is to **pleasant** as
- a. bright is to gloomy
- b. depressed is to sad
- c. posterity is to offspring
- d. weary is to upset

Ch. 8 10. detect is to **discover** as
- a. find is to keep
- b. climb is to fall
- c. detach is to loosen
- d. mangle is to tie

Test-Taking Tips

Taking a standardized test can be difficult. Here are a few things you can do to make the experience easier.

Get a good night's sleep the night before the test. You want to be alert and rested in the morning.

Eat a healthful breakfast. Good nutrition is important for brain functioning.

Wear layers of clothing. You can take off or put on a layer if you get too warm or too cold.

Bring two sharp number 2 pencils with erasers.

When you get the test, read the directions carefully. Listen to any instructions your teacher gives. Be sure you understand what you are supposed to do. If you have any questions, ask your teacher before you start marking your answers.

If you feel nervous, close your eyes and take a deep breath as you silently count to three. Then slowly breathe out. Do this several times until your mind is calm.

Manage your time. Check to see how many questions there are. Try to answer half the questions before half the time is up.

Answer the easy questions first. If you don't know the answer to a question, skip it and come back to it later if you have time.

Try to answer all the questions. Some will seem very difficult, but don't worry about it. Nobody is expected to get every answer right. Make the best guess you can. Often the first answer you think of is the correct answer.

If you make a mistake, erase it completely. Then write the correct answer or fill in the correct circle.

When you have finished, go back over the test. Work on any questions you skipped. Check your answers.

Question Types

Many tests contain the same kinds of questions. Here are a few of the question types that you may encounter.

Meaning from Context

This kind of question asks you to figure out the meaning of a word from the words or sentences around it. For example, readings might contain sentences like these.

> The tired worker trudged along the hot, dusty road.

Trudged means the worker was walking.

quickly	happily
slowly	excitedly

Read the sentence again. It says that the worker is tired, hot, and dusty. This will help you guess that *trudged* probably means the worker was walking slowly.

> These new lightbulbs are good for the earth because they conserve energy.

Which word can be substituted for *conserve*?

supply	provide
save	expand

You know that lightbulbs use energy. If the new bulbs are good for the earth, they must use less energy. The answer is *save*.

Analogy

This kind of question asks you to determine the relationship between pairs of words. Analogies usually use *is to* and *as*.

Convert is to **change** as **conceal** is to ——.

find	open
hide	depict

Convert and *change* are synonyms. They mean the same thing. Therefore, the answer is a word that means "the same as *conceal*." The answer is **hide**.

Vast is to **tiny** as **gruesome** is to ——.

ugly	beautiful
joyous	meager

Vast and *tiny* are antonyms. They mean the opposite of each other. Therefore, the answer is a word that means "the opposite of *gruesome*." The answer is **beautiful**.

Roots

This kind of question draws on your understanding of Greek and Latin roots.

Which word is based on a Latin root that means "carry."

transport	transmission
solitary	capture

You know that *sol* means "alone," and *cap* means "take," so *solitary* and *capture* are wrong. You also know that *transport* is related to words like *portable*, *export*, and *import*. They all have the meaning of "carry." You can figure out that the answer is *transport*.

Roots

Roots are the building blocks of words. Many roots come from ancient languages, such as Latin and Greek. If you know what a root means, you can often guess the meaning of a word. Some words are built by adding prefixes and suffixes to a root. Some words are formed by joining more than one root. Note that the spelling of a root can change.

Root	Language	Meaning	Examples
ast	Greek	star	astronomy, asteroid, astronaut
biblio	Greek	book	bibliography, Bible, bibliophile
cap, cep	Latin	take	capture, accept, reception
chron	Greek	time	synchronize, chronological, chronometer
geo	Greek	earth	geothermal, geochemistry, geode
meter	Greek	measure	thermometer, metric, centimeter
mis, mit	Latin	send	mission, transmit, missile
phon, phono	Greek	sound	microphone, phonics, telephone
port	Latin	carry	portable, export, report
sol	Latin	alone	solitary, solo, solitude
therm	Greek	heat	thermometer, thermal, thermostat
tort	Latin	twist	contort, torsion, torture
tract	Latin	pull	tractor, contract, traction
vac	Latin	empty	vacuum, vacancy, vacate
vid, vis	Latin	see	vision, video, visible

Prefixes

A prefix is one or more syllables added to the beginning of a word that changes the meaning of the word.

Prefix	Meaning	Examples
dis-	not, opposite of	disapprove, disappear
fore-	before, in front	forecast, foresee
il-, ir-	not	illegal, irreversible
im-	not	impatient, impossible
in-	not	inappropriate, insecure
mis-	badly, wrongly	misspell, misbehave
non-	not	nonfiction, nonviolent
over-	beyond, too much	overcharge, overflow
post-	after, later	postdate, postwar
pre-	earlier, before	prepay, prearrange
re-	again, back	reunite, restart
un-	not, opposite of	unusual, unreliable
under-	below, less than	underwater, undercooked

These prefixes indicate numbers.

Prefix	Meaning	Examples
uni-	one	unicycle, unicorn
bi-	two	bicycle, bipolar
tri-	three	triangle, trilogy
quadr-	four	quadrangle, quadruped
pent-	five	pentathlon, pentagon
dec-	ten	decimal, Decalogue
centi-	one hundred	centimeter, centipede
milli-, mill-	one thousand	millimeter, millennium
mega-	one million	megaton, megabyte
giga-	one billion	gigabyte, gigawatt

Suffixes

A suffix is one or more syllables added to the end of a word to change its meaning or to change it to a different part of speech.

Suffix	Meaning	Examples
-able, -ible	capable of being	manageable, credible
-al	relating to	natural, critical
-ant, -ent	person who	assistant, resident
-ate	to make	activate, separate
-en	to cause to	awaken, soften
-ful	full of	skillful, plentiful
-fy	to make	falsify, simplify
-hood	a condition of	adulthood, motherhood
-ic	relating to, like	athletic, poetic
-ion	act of, state of	celebration, collision
-ish	resembling, like a	childish, foolish
-ist	person who	pianist, activist
-ize	to cause to be	realize, familiarize
-like	resembling, like a	catlike, lifelike
-ment	act or process	placement, commitment
-ous	full of	courageous, dangerous
-y	full of	cloudy, foggy

Roots, Prefixes, and Suffixes

1. What does a geographer study?

   the earth

2. How many sides does a pentagon have?

   five

3. You are a job applicant. What are you doing?

   applying for a job

4. You misunderstood the directions. What did you do?

   understood them wrongly

5. How many branches does a bicameral legislature have?

   two

6. How many years are in a decade?

   ten

7. You are a bibliomaniac. What do you collect?

   books

8. The teacher clarified the directions. What did he do?

   made them clear

9. What does an astronomer study?

   the stars

10. What part of the day is the forenoon?

    the morning

11. The fog made visibility difficult. What couldn't you do well?

    see

12. What does a clownish person act like?

    a clown

13. There is a soliloquy in a play. How many actors are speaking?

    one

14. What does a chronometer measure?

    time

15. The quarterback overthrew the receiver. What did he do?

    threw too far

16. To what does a phonoreceptor respond?

    sound

17. You bought a portable computer. What can you do with it?

    carry it

18. What is in a vacant room?

    nothing

19. How many years are in a century?

    100

20. How many years are in a millennium?

1,000

21. What does a metallic substance contain?

metal

22. How many volts are in a megavolt?

a million

23. What would a tortuous path be like?

twisty

24. What does a thermometer do?

measure heat

25. The afternoon was uneventful. What happened?

nothing

26. How many feet does a quadruped have?

four

27. The dentist extracted the bad tooth. What did she do to it?

pulled it out

28. You read "Please remit payment" on a bill. What should you do with the money?

send it in

29. You bought a nonreturnable shirt. What can't you do with it?

return it

30. How many legs does a tripod have?

three

Word Cube

Categories: *Partners, Visual Learners*

Work with a partner. You will each need a sheet of paper, a pencil, tape, and a pair of scissors. Each of you chooses six of the current chapter's vocabulary words and makes a Word Cube. To make a Word Cube, draw six squares in a shape like this on the paper.

Write in each square one of the vocabulary words you chose. Then cut along the outside lines. Fold and tape the sides of the shape to make a cube. Take turns rolling the cubes. To score a point, write a sentence that makes sense, using the two words that were rolled. The first player to get five points wins the game.

Vocabulary Commercials

Categories: *Small Group, Technology*

Work with two partners. You will need several sheets of paper and a pencil. On one sheet of paper, list the vocabulary words from the current chapter. Then make a list of things you use every day—a bowl, cereal, shoes, and so on. Choose one of the items you listed and write a TV commercial to advertise that product. Write a script that lets all three partners play a role. Use at least 10 of the vocabulary words from the current chapter in your commercial. Practice acting out your commercial. Share your commercial with the class by making a video or by presenting a skit.

Creating Categories

Category: *Small Group*

Find two partners. You will each need a sheet of paper and a pencil. Each partner writes three of the current chapter's vocabulary words that are related in some way. For example, you might list words that are all used to describe people, that are all nouns, or that all describe ways to move from place to place. Challenge your partners to guess the connection between the words you listed.

Conducting Interviews

Categories: *Partners, Technology*

Work with a partner. You will need a sheet of paper and a pencil. One partner will be a news reporter and interview the other. The reporter writes questions to ask in the interview. The questions should contain at least 10 of the vocabulary words from the current chapter. The person being interviewed answers the questions, using vocabulary words if possible. When the interview is complete, switch places and let the other partner write questions and conduct an interview. If possible, record your interview on audio or video to share with the class.

Crack the Number Code

Categories: *Partners, ELL*

With a partner, write 10 sentences using the current chapter's vocabulary words. Next, assign a number to each letter of the alphabet (A=1, B=2, C=3, and so on). Code all the words in your sentences with the numbers you have assigned. For example, the code for the sentence "The cat sat on a mat" would be the following:

20, 8, 5 + 3, 1, 20 + 19, 1, 20 + 15, 14 + 1 + 13, 1, 20

Once you have coded all the sentences, exchange papers with another group and try to "crack the code." The first team to figure out all the sentences wins the game.

Crossword Puzzle

Categories: *Individual, Visual Learners*

Prepare for the game by bringing to class crossword puzzles from newspapers or magazines. Use these examples as a guide to create a crossword puzzle using the current chapter's vocabulary words. The word clues for "across" and "down" will be the vocabulary word definitions. Use graph paper for the crossword grid.

When finished, exchange puzzles with a friend and complete it. Return the crossword puzzle to its owner to check for accuracy.

Vocabulary Board Games

Categories: *Partners, Visual Learners*

Find a partner and discuss types of board games you like to play. Talk about the object of the game, the rules, and the equipment needed. Then create a Vocabulary Board Game. Think of a way to include the current chapter's vocabulary words in the game. For example, the vocabulary words could be written on word cards. When a player lands on a certain square, he or she must draw a card and define the word.

Create a game board on an open manila folder. Find or make game pieces, and write a list of game rules. Exchange Vocabulary Board Games with classmates and play their games. Keep the board games in a designated spot in the classroom and adapt the vocabulary cards for each new chapter.

All About Alliteration

Category: *Small Group*

Alliteration is the repetition of initial sounds within a sentence. Work in groups of three or four to create alliterative sentences that contain the current chapter's vocabulary words. The only words that can be used that do not start with the initial letter are *and, in, of, the, a,* and *an.* The object of the game is to see which group can come up with the longest sentence. (It can be silly, but it must make sense.) For example, using the vocabulary word *timid:*

The tremendously timid tiger tossed twelve tasteless trees toward the terrified turtle.

Word Sorts

Categories: *Small Group,*
Visual Learners

Work with a partner. Divide a sheet of paper into four sections labeled *Nouns, Adjectives, Adverbs,* and *Verbs*. Write each of the current chapter's vocabulary words in the appropriate section. When you and your partner feel that you have successfully placed each word in the appropriate box, turn your activity sheet upside down. (Allow only three minutes to complete this step.)

When the time has elapsed, exchange activity sheets with another pair and check for accuracy. (Use your *Vocabulary in Action* book for clarification.) The pair of partners with the most correct answers wins the game.

For an additional challenge, change the part of speech of the vocabulary words by using prefixes and suffixes. For example, if the vocabulary word is *migration,* you could add the verb *migrate* and the adjective *migratory.*

Good News, Bad News

Categories: *Individual,*
Partner

Write a good news and bad news letter to a friend or relative. Alternate sentences that begin "The good news is" with sentences that begin "The bad news is." Use one of the current chapter's vocabulary words in each "good news" sentence. Use an antonym of that vocabulary word in the "bad news" sentence. For example, if the word is *compliment,* you might write "The good news is I received a compliment from my teacher for doing a nice job on my research paper. The bad news is I gave my teacher an insult when I forgot to say "thank you."

For an extra challenge, leave blank spaces for the antonyms and exchange papers with a friend to complete.

Proofread Pen Pals

Category: *Small Group*

Find a friend and work together to write a friendly letter that includes at least six of the current chapter's vocabulary words. Your letter can be about school, sports, friends, family, or any other interesting topic. (Use a resource book to help you with the correct form for a friendly letter.) Include errors in your letter, such as spelling, punctuation, capitalization, and word meaning.

When you have completed your letter, exchange it with another pair of partners. Correct the new letter. After all the corrections have been made, return the letter to the original owners. They will make sure all the errors have been found.

Vocabulary Dominoes

Categories: *Small Group,*
ELL

Begin the game by writing all the current chapter's vocabulary words on index cards. Write the definitions of the words on other index cards.

Place all the index cards facedown in the center of the playing area. This will be the domino bank. Each player chooses four dominoes as his or her supply. Turn one domino faceup to begin play. The object of the game is to match the words with their definitions.

If Player 1 makes a match, he or she places the two cards down on the table, and Player 2 chooses. If Player 1 doesn't make a match, he or she must take a new domino from the bank. If that domino doesn't match either, the player must add it to his or her supply. Player 2 then tries to make a match. The first player to match all the dominoes in his or her supply is the winner.

Impromptu Stories

Category: *Small Group*

Write each of the current chapter's vocabulary word on an index card. Shuffle the cards and place them facedown in a deck. Players take turns drawing five cards from the deck. As each player draws cards, he or she makes up a story using the words on the five cards. Players can use any form of the word listed. To make the activity more challenging, try to make the players' stories build on one another.

Vocabulary Sayings

Category: *Small Group*

Find three partners. Write down the following five sayings:

Birds of a feather flock together.

A rolling stone gathers no moss.

Too many cooks spoil the broth.

A penny saved is a penny earned.

A stitch in time saves nine.

Then brainstorm other sayings. When your list is complete, rewrite the ending of each saying, using a vocabulary word from the current chapter. Example: Birds of a feather sit on our overhang.

Try to create two new endings for each saying. Share your list with other groups or create a class bulletin-board display of your work.

One-Sided Phone Conversations

Categories: *Small Group, Auditory Learners*

Find a partner. Work together to write one person's side of a phone conversation. Use at least 10 vocabulary words from the current chapter. Be sure to include both questions and answers in the conversation. When you have finished, find another pair of students with whom to work. Read your one-sided conversation to the other pair. After you read each sentence or question, ask them to fill in what the person on the other side of the conversation might have said. Then listen to the other pair's conversation and do the same. Try to use vocabulary words as you create the second side of the phone conversation.

Mystery Word Web

Categories: *Small Group, Visual Learners*

Find three partners. Draw a word web on a sheet of paper or on the board. One partner chooses a vocabulary word from the current chapter and fills in the outer circles of the web with clues about the word. The other partners try to guess which word is being suggested. Each partner should take at least two turns describing a word. Be sure to include the Challenge Words in the activity.

Vocabulary Answer and Question

Category: *Large Group*

Gather these materials: poster board, 20 index cards, a list of the current chapter's vocabulary words and definitions, tape. Tape the tops of the index cards to the poster board so that they form five columns of four cards. Under each index card, write a vocabulary word. Divide into two teams and line up in two rows facing each other. Flip a coin to see which team goes first.

The first player chooses and removes an index card, revealing the word beneath it. The team has 20 seconds to provide the definition of the word in question form. For example, if the word *usurp* is revealed, a correct response would be "What is 'to seize power from an individual or a group'?" If a correct definition is given, the team scores a point and the next player in line takes a turn. If an incorrect definition is given, play passes to the other team. The first person in line chooses a new index card. Play continues until all the cards have been removed. The team that gives the greater number of correct definitions wins.

Dictionary Dash

Category: *Small Group*

Find three partners and divide into two teams. You will need a dictionary, a sheet of paper, and a pencil. Write 10 vocabulary words on index cards and place them facedown on the floor. The first team turns over a card to reveal one of the vocabulary words. Each team should then look up the word in the dictionary and record the following

information about the vocabulary word on a sheet of paper:

how many different definitions the word has

the correct pronunciation

the guide words located on the dictionary page

a sentence that uses the word correctly

When both teams have finished, exchange papers and check for accuracy. The team that finishes first and has no mistakes receives two points. If the other team makes no mistakes, it receives one point. The game continues until all vocabulary index cards have been turned over. The team with the most points wins the game.

Vocabulary Haiku

Category: *Individual*

The word *haiku* comes from two Japanese words that mean "play" and "poem." A haiku is a poem that contains 17 syllables. It is written in a three-line format. The first line has five syllables, the second has seven syllables, and the third has five syllables. Frequently, a haiku describes a scene in nature.

Using the current chapter's vocabulary words, create your own haiku. For example, here is a haiku for the vocabulary word *harmonize*:

Soft falling raindrops
Harmonize with the children
Playing in the rain.

When the class has created several haiku, collect them and create a book. You may also wish to read your poems aloud to the class.

Word Wizards

Category: *Small Group*

Find three partners and divide into two teams. Choose one of the current chapter's vocabulary words. Each pair of partners writes the word at the top of a sheet of paper. The object of the game is to write as many forms of the word as possible by adding prefixes, suffixes, and word endings. For example, using the word *scribe,* you could write these words: *scriber, scribing, script, prescribe, subscription, subscribed, scribed, subscriber, subscript, subscribes, subscribe, subscribing.*

Each round should last three minutes. At the completion of a round, teams exchange papers and check for accuracy. Use a dictionary to clarify any questions.

For each correct word form, one point is awarded. For example, the above list would receive 12 points. Use a new vocabulary word for each round. The team with the most points at the end wins.

Captions

Categories: *Small Group,*
**   *Visual Learners***

Find two partners. You will need old newspapers or magazines, scissors, paper, and glue or tape. Clip five pictures from the newspapers or magazines. Write a caption for each picture that describes what is being shown. Include at least one vocabulary word from the current chapter in each caption. Attach the captions to the photos and display them in the room.

Vocabulary Charades

Categories: *Small Group,*
**   *Kinesthetic Learners***

Find three partners. Write on a slip of paper each vocabulary word from the current chapter. Fold the slips and drop them into a box. Partners take turns selecting words and acting them out. The actor may not make any sounds. The first person to guess the word earns a point.

Password

Category: *Small Group*

Find three partners and divide into two pairs. Write on a slip of paper each vocabulary word from a chapter. Divide the slips evenly between the teams. One partner will be the "giver" and the other the "receiver." The giver views the word on the first slip and gives the receiver a one-word clue about it. The receiver tries to guess the word. If he or she is correct, the giver goes to the next slip of paper. If the receiver is wrong, the giver gives another one-word clue. If the receiver does not guess the word after three clues, the giver goes to the next word. The team has three minutes to cover as many words as possible. A point is awarded for each correct answer. The second team then has three minutes to go through its words.

Pledges

Categories: *Partners, Visual Learners*

Work with a partner. Think of ways to improve your school or community. Write a pledge that lists the things you will do to make improvements. Use vocabulary words from the current chapter. Make an illustrated bulletin board of class pledges.

Step Up Vocabulary

Categories: *Large Group, Kinesthetic Learners*

Have the class form a line along one side of the room. Designate a "goal line" about 15 feet away. Ask players in turn appropriate questions about the current chapter's vocabulary words. For example:

What is the definition of (the vocabulary word)?

Use (the vocabulary word) correctly in a sentence.

What is a synonym for (the vocabulary word)?

What is an antonym for (the vocabulary word)?

What is the root word of (the vocabulary word)?

Name three forms of (the vocabulary word)?

What is the present/past/future tense of (the vocabulary word)?

If the player correctly answers a question, he or she may advance one step toward the goal line. The first player to reach the goal line is the winner.

Word Volleyball

Category: *Large Group*

Divide the class into two teams and have them line up facing each other. Toss a coin to see which team goes first. Say one of the current chapter's vocabulary words. The first person on Team 1 must provide a synonym for the word. Then, like in the game of volleyball, the word is sent back to Team 2. The first person on that team must provide another synonym for the word.

Play continues until one team cannot provide a correct synonym. The team that provides the last correct synonym scores a point. Say a new word and continue with the next player. This game can also be played using antonyms.

Class Debate

Categories: *Small Group, Technology*

Divide the class into an even number of teams of four or five debaters. Give pairs of teams the pro or con side of issues they may feel strongly about. For example:

TV has nothing good to offer.

Students should wear school uniforms.

Everyone should learn a foreign language.

Allow 10 minutes for teams to prepare their arguments. Each team must use at least three of the current chapter's vocabulary words in its presentation. Have the teams present their arguments to the class. Have the class choose the winner of each debate. You might make a video of the debates so the students can see themselves.

Listen to This

Categories: *Individual,*
Auditory Learners,
ELL,
Technology

Some English-language learners may be more proficient in oral than in written English. Record each of the current chapter's vocabulary words followed by a slight pause and then its definition. Let individuals listen to the complete recording several times. Then have them listen to each word, stop the recorder, and define the word themselves. They can then listen to the definition to make sure they were correct.

Same and Opposite

Category: *Small Group*

Use this activity for reinforcement or reteaching. Write on index cards each of the current chapter's vocabulary words.

Write a synonym and an antonym for each word on separate cards. Shuffle the synonym and antonym cards and place them facedown on a table. Distribute the vocabulary word cards evenly among a small group of students. One student turns over the first card in the pile. Players must look at their vocabulary words to see if that card is a synonym or antonym of the word on the first card. If it is, he or she takes the card and places it faceup on the table with its matching vocabulary card. Continue until all the cards have been matched. The player with the most matched sets of three wins.

What's the Word?

Category: *Large Group*

Write each of the current chapter's vocabulary words on an index card or self-stick note and display them on a bulletin board. Tell the students to try to use the words during the day. When a student uses a word in an appropriate way, he or she gets to take the card. See who has the most cards at the end of the day.

Here is a list of all the words defined in this book. The number following each word indicates the page on which the word is defined. The Challenge Words are listed in *italics*. The Word Study words are listed in **bold**.

impact, 20
impede, 87
implement, 29
incomplete, 153
incomprehensible, 44
inconsistent, 59
independent, 153
indispensable, 137
induce, 54
inept, 63
inevitable, 77
infamous, 25
inflict, 161
ingenious, 165
initiative, 87
inquire, 98
insinuate, 49
insistent, 127
integrate, 155
interrogate, 151
invalid, 122
invigorate, 111
irrational, 122
irregular, 132
irreversible, 153
irritable, 145

jovial, 165
joyous, 119
judicious, 10
juvenile, 20

keen, 30

lame, 171
lavish, 59
lax, 161
legacy, 15
legislate, 44
leisure, 54
liberate, 63
literal, 78
livelihood, 41
lubricate, 137

magnitude, 83
malady, 171
malignant, 171
mangle, 87
manipulate, 98
mar, 69
marine, 112
maul, 122
meager, 35
melancholy, 151
mental, 132
metallic, 146
meteoric, 155
miniature, 166
mischievous, 10
misdemeanor, 25
misfit, 20
mismanage, 30

monologue, 61
monorail, 61
motherhood, 41

nautical, 156
negligent, 156
negotiate, 64
neighborhood, 41
neutral, 166
nobility, 44
nomad, 54
nonabrasive, 78
nostalgia, 103
notation, 30
nullify, 156

obligation, 64
obscure, 78
observation, 87
obstacle, 98
oddly, 112
ointment, 122
oppress, 127
oracle, 132
orthodox, 103
ovation, 146
overcharge, 129
overcooked, 129
overflow, 129
overload, 129
overpay, 129
overseas, 27
oversees, 27
oversleep, 129

pacifist, 156
paradox, 93
parallel, 112
parcel, 166
parody, 10
patronize, 117
peaceful, 7
pedestal, 54
pedestrian, 78
pending, 137
perch, 20
perishable, 30
perspective, 98
persuasion, 88
pervade, 151
photographic, 75
physical, 44
pigment, 54
pioneer, 64
plight, 59
pore, 78
portable, 51
portage, 51
portfolio, 51
postdate, 85
posterity, 88
postgraduate, 85

postpone, 85
postscript, 85
posttest, 85
postwar, 85
powerful, 7
precaution, 98
prescribe, 49
presume, 112
prevail, 122
prevention, 132
principle, 146
procedure, 30
procure, 117
proficient, 15
profit, 156
prudent, 35
puncture, 166
pupil, 10

quaint, 161
qualm, 20
quench, 30

radiant, 44
radioactivity, 54
rage, 64
react, 78
rebel, 88
receipt, 163
receive, 163
reception, 163
recuperate, 98
regime, 83
relations, 112
reliance, 122
report, 51
reservoir, 132
resign, 146
retaliate, 156
retreat, 166
reveal, 10
ridiculous, 119

savage, 30
scant, 44
scenic, 156
schedule, 146
scholar, 54
scoundrel, 64
serene, 78
shaft, 88
shed, 98
sheen, 44
shrill, 112
signify, 122
simmer, 132
simulate, 146
slander, 166
slogan, 10
smolder, 20
sneer, 30
solitary, 44
sparse, 54

spectrum, 64
splendor, 64
sprawl, 78
stalemate, 151
stamina, 88
stifle, 161
stir, 98
strenuous, 112
stupefy, 122
sturdy, 132
submissive, 146
successful, 7
suspicious, 119
swindle, 156

technical, 166
tedious, 20
tendency, 166
tendon, 10
tension, 20
terminal, 30
thoughtful, 7
timid, 88
transcribe, 151
transport, 51
triangle, 61
tricolor, 61
tricycle, 61
trifle, 44
triumph, 54
trudge, 64
turmoil, 25

unicellular, 61
unique, 171
unscathed, 137
uphold, 78
urban, 88
utmost, 93

valiant, 98
variable, 112
variation, 122
vast, 132
veil, 146
velocity, 156
vengeance, 171
verge, 166
vibrate, 10
vigilant, 103
vital, 20
vocation, 30
volume, 44
voluntary, 54

warrant, 64
weave, 78
whisk, 88
wholesome, 98
wistful, 112
wondrous, 122
wrangle, 132
writhe, 146

Index of Words   Level F